I0007048

Microsoft Dynamics AX 2012

A book

on

Sales Process

Marius Popescu

Copyright © 2014 Marius POPESCU

All rights reserved.

ISBN: **1470055627**
ISBN-13: **978-1470055622**

DEDICATION

To my son Matei Constantin and my beautiful wife Simona.

CONTENTS

PREFACE

The present book is the first in a series of books dedicated to Microsoft's new ERP Dynamics AX 2012, covering the Sales and Receivables areas. The target audience consists of those individuals involved in the implementation of the ERP, both consultants and customers, but also to students interested in ERP. It represents my current understanding and description of these functionalities and how to use them in order to provide the right solutions to new or existing issues in businesses where AX is or will be implemented. I would like to make this book better, so please feel free to send me your feedback to my email address ax.mariuspopescu@yahoo.com.

CHAPTER 1
SALES BUSINESS PROCESSES

Perhaps no other area of business activity gives rise to as much discussion among and between those directly involved and those who are not involved as the activity known as sales or selling, with the related account receivables activities. This is not surprising when one considers that so many people derive their livelihood, either directly or indirectly, from selling. Even those who have no direct involvement in selling come into contact with it in their roles as consumers.

The ERP must support the sales operations and the sales department (and other departments) with out-of-the-box functionality, but also has to be flexible enough to handle/model new situations coming from the day-to-day operations. The primary responsibility of sales and distribution is to provide customers with your goods and services, when they need it and where they need it. In order to fulfill this task, sales and distribution needs to manage material requirements of customers by processing sales orders through picking, shipping and invoicing.

These customer requirements may originate from one or more order streams, such as direct customer communication with order entry personnel, sales representatives, web-placed orders, EDI, etc.

Business

Microsoft Dynamics AX 2012 supports a variety of order entry scenarios to fulfill numerous business requirements. The focus of these scenarios ranges from tightly integrated collaborative business-to-business relations that use the Application Integration Framework (AIF), to customers on the self-service portal, sales representatives on the Enterprise Portal, and users who perform Microsoft Dynamics AX 2012 client-based order entry when a sales order is processed.

Before we start to go through the details, the lines below should give an overall picture of business processes in sales and distribution.

Starting point for sales and distribution is correct master data, in particular customer-related and item-related data.

At sales quotation and/or sales order creation, master data copy to transaction data. Sales quotations and sales orders therefore receive customer and item data as a default, with customer data in the header of the order and the item related data on each line. You may modify these default data in transactions, as an example if your customer requests a different delivery address or has requested and agreed a different payment term. If such a modification applies for future orders as well, you should change the customer record, which contains the appropriate master data in this case.

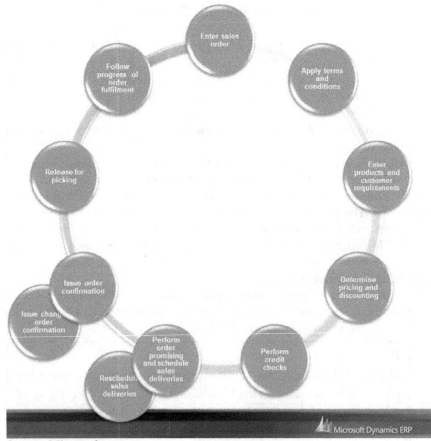

Source: Microsoft

Following customer request, the sales representative may present a sales quotation (or several alternative sales quotations). The quotation may be created for a prospect or an existing customer. A sales quotation consists of a header, which primarily contains customer/prospect data, and one or more lines, which contain the ordered items. However, in order to automatically create a sales order from a sales quotation, the prospect needs to be transformed into a customer (as mentioned before, we need master data).

Note: Depending on the starting point of the sales flow, different roles in the company may be involved. As you probably know, Microsoft Dynamics AX 2012 is built to provide increased productivity to employees and the central point of this approach is the Role Center[1] - a personalized page for each functional role in the company.

Enter sales order

A sales order may be registered manually or may be created automatically, as the result of transforming a sales quotation into a sales order. Other possible source for a sales order may be sales agreements.

> **Business**
>
> In distribution companies it is a common practice to view customer sales history at order entry.
>
> **Usability**
>
> When a customer is selected for the creation of an order the fact box that is displayed on the right hand side of the form will display past sales orders. The related fact box will display a summary of Open Quotations, Open Sales orders, Open customer invoices, Open return orders. The operator can click on any of these statistics to drill into and see the details of the open and history documents. Additionally the user can enter the customer account associated with the sales order to drill into the customer master record. From here the operator can see all transaction history related to the customer. It's important to note that the information displayed to the order entry operator is controlled by the security roles associated with the user.

Apply terms and conditions

The default terms and conditions from the customer record are copied to the sales order header.

---

[1] The Microsoft Dynamics Role Tailored user interface includes more than 30 Role Centers and makes it easy for everyone in key business areas to access and share self-service business intelligence (BI) and reporting.

Enter products and customer requirements

If specific conditions are required by the customer for a sales order, the default terms and conditions may be changed at order entry.

Also when adding items on sales order lines the default item settings are copied/determined from item record and the system takes into account the existing trade agreements to determine the applicable prices and discounts.

Determine pricing and discounting

Prices and discounts are determined from trade agreements. Trade agreements are a matrix pricing/discount list system. Trade agreement creation and updates are made through the trade agreement journals. Through the journal all fields associated with pricing can be updated. The journal can handle updates to purchase and sales prices, line discounts, multi-line discounts and total discounts. Using the select feature the operation can select which type of agreement update is being done, which customers, vendors, items or date ranges. The journal has multiple features, such as copy line, clear journal or delete lines. Using the Adjustment process an update can be processed based on percentage or amount to update. Dynamics AX introduces concepts as generic currency and smart rounding for powerful multi-currency support. Attributes that can be included in a trade agreement include customer code or customer group, item code or item group, currency, quantity range, lead time, from/to date, unit of measure, item configuration, item size, item color, site, warehouse, batch number, location, serial number.

Business

In distribution companies it is essential to have a clear pricing and discounting policy and also the possibility to bulk process the item sales prices.

Determine credit checks

Dynamics AX 2012 offers credit limit functionality that can determine if a customer can order additional merchandise. Depending on requirements, the system can consider items on orders in different stages when computing the credit. It is also the user's choice if the system should only warn (warning message) or should prevent (error message) on entering new transactions when the credit limit is exceeded.

Perform order promising and schedule sales deliveries

Available-to-promise can automatically or manually be performed during order line entry and order line change. For each product it is possible to define the default order promising method: sales lead time, ATP, CTP. Using

ATP, a single sales order demand will not trigger a new purchase/production order; the demand from the order line relies on what is already on-hand or planned based on forecast. The ATP calculation applies a time phased approach, looking at the cumulative projected available inventory, which may include existing planned orders and safety margin. ATP does not suggest new planned orders. However CTP may suggest a new planned order, such as a work order based on the supply policy for the product. Similarly to ATP, the CTP (Capable-to-Promise) calculation applies a time phased approach, considering the product's supply policy, projected available material, and capacity constraints for the bill of materials and route definition of a product. When using CTP, the order processor lets CTP calculate the earliest feasible ship date by performing a Microsoft Dynamics AX explosion of the line item's bill of materials. View Chapter 5 – Sales Order for detailed information about ATP and CTP considerations.

Issue order confirmation/Issue change order confirmation
The sales entry user has the ability to confirm an order by clicking the sales order confirmation button. For each change made after a confirmation is posted, the system requires a new confirmation. There is a confirmation history available for each sales order. If there is a need to re-print the confirmation then users can click on the Sales order confirmation button in the order header which will display a list of posted confirmations. Through this form the user can preview or print a copy.

Release for picking
In order to ship the item, you may print a picking list to prepare delivery. The internal shipment procedure, meaning the internal company's warehouse(s) operations, is finished when a packing slip posts. The packing slip reduces the physical quantity in inventory as well as the open sales order quantity. You may post a packing slip without previously posting a picking list, if your company does not need picking lists.

Follow progress on sales order fulfillment
System allows the tracking of a sales order fulfillment through the sales order line status and the deliver reminder functionality. Back orders are evaluated and can be used as an indicator for sales order fulfillment and customer satisfaction.

After posting the packing slip, you may post an invoice. If you do not require a separate packing slip, you may as well post the invoice without a previous packing slip. In this case, the invoice posts the physical and the financial transaction in parallel.

If you want to record a sales invoice referring to a service instead of an item, you may choose to enter a free text invoice. In the lines of a free text invoice, you select ledger account numbers (termed main accounts in Dynamics AX 2012) instead of item numbers.

Payment Processing

Although this is not really a sales process step, the last part of a sales consists of invoice payment. Even if the sales personnel considers the sales made, your company may be interested more in actual sales amount receiving. In some companies this approach reflects the way the commission is paid, e.g. the commission is paid at full invoice payment. You expect your customer to pay the invoice before the due date with or without cash discount deduction. If the customer does not pay the invoice meeting in the terms of payment, you may process payment reminders in Dynamics AX or you can use the new Collection functionality to analyze and manage bad debt.

Some additional aspects involved with the sales process are commission calculation, inquiries and reports used for daily activities.

Because of the deep integration of Dynamics AX, all inventory and customer transactions in sales and distribution post to ledger accounts in parallel.

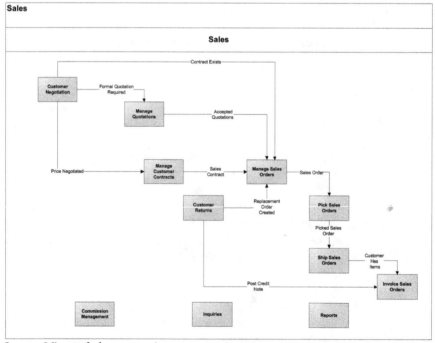

Source: Microsoft documentation
AX 2012 Sales Overview

2 CUSTOMERS IN DYNAMICS AX 2012

Each sales transaction must be associated with a customer. Customer information is maintained per legal entity and can have unlimited addresses, contact information (such as phone numbers and e-mail) and contact people associated to it. It includes but not limited to information such as payment terms and schedule, discounts (line, multi-line or total discounts), credit limit, shipping method, delivery terms, typical delivery method, and financial dimensions. All of these values can be defined on the customer record and used as defaults to quotations, sales orders, and invoices. Customization is available to define the criteria for any new or existing field of the customer record.

Defining Customers
Use the Customer form (Sales and Marketing->Common->Customers-> All customers or Accounts receivable->Common->Customers-> All customers) to create, maintain and inquire about customers. Enter as much data as possible in advance, because the data is used throughout the system for invoicing, payments, reports and the base data is automatically displayed as the default for all transactions that involve the customer. You can change default information at any time. To expedite the process of creating customers, you can create templates[2] based on the entries in the fields of specific customers that you specify as template models.
Templates can be used by all users or a single user. If a template is available when you create a new customer, a form appears that displays the available customer templates. Select the template that applies to the new customer. The

---

[2] Templates can be used to default values when creating customer records. An unlimited number of templates can be defined by the organization and each user.

field values of the template are copied into the fields of the new customer. You can make changes to the fields and enter more information, as appropriate.

System identifies customers using Customer account, which is a unique identifier per legal entity. However, the system manages the same customer across organization (see picture below).

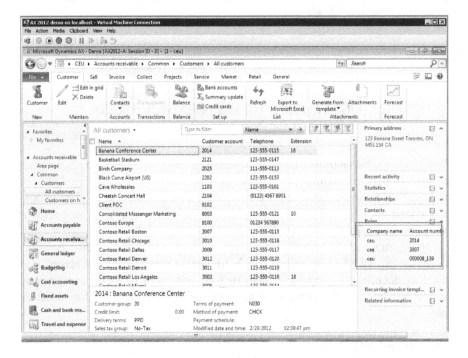

The customer account has a default size of 20 characters (although it can be modified with customization). The field can be divided into segments using the number sequence definitions.

Customers are created from the Accounts receivable menu, click Common, click Customers, and then click All customers. When user clicks New->Customer in the action pane, the Customer – New record form is shown.

The system automatically generates the Customer account if the customer account number sequence is specified in the Accounts receivable parameters form in the Number sequences section.

The red underlined fields are mandatory fields, representing the minimum information that the system needs to consider a new record valid. Besides the Name and Country/region, the most important mandatory information is the Customer group field, used to set up automatic posting to General Ledger accounts for revenue generated by customers and cost of goods sold, but also to enable default settings on customer record (see the Usability text box below).

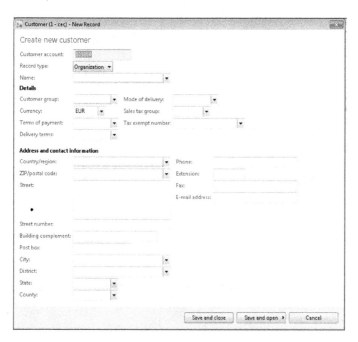

There are multiple options available on the customer creation form that can optimize operations when all details for the new customer are entered. The default option is Save and close, which saves the record for future references, without any consequent action. The other options are accessed through the Save and open button, as following:

- Customer – saves the record and open it in the Customer form
- Sales quotation – saves the record and creates a new sales quotation for this customer
- Sales Order - saves the record and creates a new sales order for this customer
- Project quotation - saves the record and creates a new project quotation for this customer

To prevent accidental change, a new Edit button was added on Customer form to enable or disable editing[3].

---

[3] The Edit Functionality is a general new feature in Microsoft Dynamics AX 2012.

> **Usability**
> When selecting the customer group, the values of certain fields in the Customer groups form are automatically copied to the customer account. The included fields are:
> o Terms of payment
> o Settle period
> o Item posting ledger accounts, including the Sales tax group account.

The language selected in the Language field is used for all external documents. You can use this code to display item description translations or to print documents like packing slips or invoices in that selected language. Translations are provided for the 42 languages[4] provided with Microsoft Dynamics AX 2012. The language code is mandatory and it defaults from the Company information form.

Customer's Addresses and Contact Information
In the Customers form, on the Addresses and Contact information FastTab, user can enter the customer address and contact details.

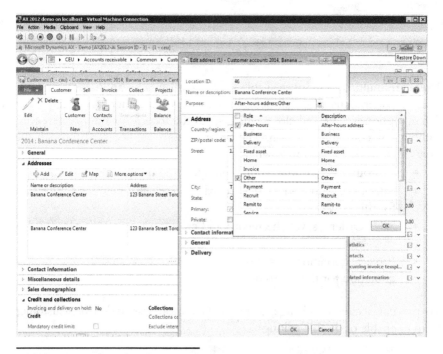

---

[4] Microsoft is continuously updating the languages available, so this information is subject to change at any time.

A customer can have more than one address, such as business, invoice, delivery, or payment address entered by clicking the Add button and entering the relevant information in the Edit address window. A Map button displays the address position on map, if parameters like latitude and longitude exists.

> **Business**
>
> In some cases there may be the case for customers with multiple delivery addresses in different states or countries, which may require entering of the appropriate tax group for each alternative address.

One-time customers

There are cases when sales to a customer will not reoccur in the future and the company does not want to keep in the system information about that customer (for example, some types of retail businesses only require a generic customer). Select the One-time customer check box to indicate if the company only deals with this customer one time.

This feature may be enabled from Accounts Receivables parameters form, where a default customer account number can be specified. This will serve as a default template for one-time customers, which information will be copied automatically to a newly created customer record (a number sequence must be supplied for one-time customers from which the new customer ID is generated) when creating a sale to a one-time customer in the Create sales order dialog window. User has to supply the customer's name.

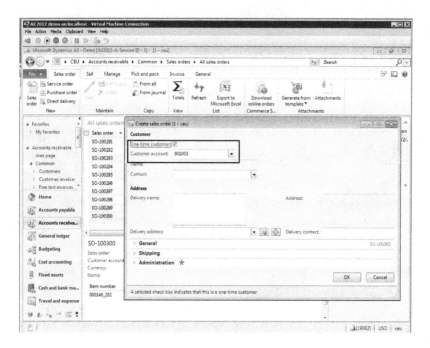

Other miscellaneous customer details

Select a statistical group in the Statistics group list to make reports and statistics about this customer. For example, the statistics group may be used to prioritize customers based on their importance.

Another important feature used by accounts receivable clerk is the ability to specify the frequency of when you send the customer an account statement by using the Account statement list. Depending on companies' policies, this can be monthly, determined by the Always option, every three months, using Quarter option, every six months (Biannually), once per year (Annually) or Never.

Depending on the selection in the Address book type field on the General FastTab, in the Government identification area you may enter values in the ID number, Country/region, or State fields. These government-established data values are commonly used to protect companies against financial loss due to delinquent accounts.

Select a vendor account number in the Vendor account field if the customer is also a vendor for your organization. Use the vendor account for reimbursement - if a customer has a credit amount because of overpayment or a credit note, you can transfer the amount to the vendor account.

Credit and Collections customer details

Dynamics AX provides a credit check feature which can be enabled with the Credit rating parameters in the Accounts Receivables module. These parameters provide a way to enable Check of credit limit on sales order, a message when credit limit is exceeded, credit limit type for example. On the customer master record you have the option of specifying the credit rating and a limit. When the user is posting transactions through the Sales and Marketing module if these parameters are set then a credit limit check will be performed. The user also has the option of performing a credit check when posting by setting the Check Credit limit option on the posting parameters.

Set up credit and collections information for the customer by selecting whether invoicing or deliveries have been placed on hold for the customer.

- No: all transactions are possible.
- Invoice: the main account is blocked for everything before Invoice. Money can still be received, and an invoice can be sent on goods delivered before the blocking.
- All: all transactions are on hold.
- Payment: payment transactions are on hold.
- Requisition: requisitions transactions are on hold.
- Never: never allow the transactions to be placed on hold.

Select the Mandatory credit limit check box to check for exceeded credit limits and, if found, to display an error message. In the Credit limit field, enter the maximum outstanding amount allowed in the balance of the customer's account. This amount is always stated in the default currency.

In the Credit rating field, enter the credit rating of the customer. It is used only for statistical purposes.

Enter appropriate collections information in the following fields:

- Collections contact
- Include interest charges
- Exclude collections fees

Invoice and Delivery customer information

There are cases when the sell-to and bill-to customers are not the same. We can use the Invoice account field to link several customers to one invoice account. If there is more than one customer who has the same payment address, or if the customer's account is paid through a third party, then the invoice account is where the invoice amount is credited. If you leave the Invoice account field blank, the system uses the customer account number by default.

The delivery terms, mode of delivery, receipt calendar can be specified in the Delivery area. This information will default to the sales order header. The destination code field can be used to divide deliveries into groups according to customer's location.

13

Specify whether tax should be calculated on the invoice in the Sales tax group field. Select the Prices include sales tax check box to ensure that you include sales tax when you inform customers about sales prices, unless they want the prices excluding sales taxes (for example, prices excluding VAT). Also enter the Tax exempt number and Packing duty license number fields.

Customer Payment Information

Enter information about how to manage payments on the invoices entered in Accounts Receivable in the Customer form, on the Payment FastTab. The following payment information can be entered:

- Terms of payment
- Method of payment
- Payment specification
- Payment schedule. A payment schedule can be associated with the terms of payment which is associated with the customer. There is no limit to the number of payment schedules that can be setup. The payment schedule is user defined and can specify if the payment is a fixed number of payments over a period, fixed quantity, specific amounts as needed.
- Payment day
- Cash discount. A cash discount is used as an incentive for customers that pay before due date.
- Bank account
- Bank account number

Customer Financial Dimensions

Set up specific financial dimensions for a customer on the Financial Dimensions FastTab. Throughout the system, you can use financial dimensions to group data in different ways. If you designate financial dimensions for a customer, those financial dimensions automatically default for transactions for that customer. You can change these defaulted values when you enter the transaction. Financial dimensions enable sales analysis by customer type and, used with other entities such as items, sales persons, sales campaigns, etc. to provide multi-dimensional analysis.

The Financial Dimensions feature is a very important part of Dynamics AX 2012 that can be creatively used to provide more detailed description of transactions, simplify the accounting process, analyze and classify financial transactions, enable viewing data from different perspectives since they can be used throughout the system.

3 PRODUCTS IN DYNAMICS AX 2012

The other part/master data involved in a sales transaction is the product or the sales category[5] sold. Product information management in Microsoft Dynamics® AX 2012 is another name for the creation and maintenance of an Enterprise Products Repository. It supports larger organizations in a centralized, structured approach in creating and maintaining core master data such as product definitions. Smaller organizations that require a more decentralized approach can, with some restrictions, create and maintain their respective products while their products are automatically added to the shared products repository. Throughout this chapter the presentation will be made in parallel for Microsoft Dynamics AX 2009 and Microsoft Dynamics AX 2012 versions, in order to better reflect the new approach in the last version.

Defining products
As the Product is the central master data for managing supply chain activities and inventory management in distribution and/or manufacturing environments, the information provided must be complete and has to satisfy requirements from areas such as sales, purchasing, warehouse management, accounting and financials, manufacturing, quality management and logistics, industry standards, intercompany operations.
In Dynamics AX 2012, Microsoft has enhanced the item-product data management framework to provide flexibility and sustainability across the organization. To accomplish the new functionality, the data model was completely reworked, making many of the core item master tables shared. A

---

[5] If creating a sales order not referring to a clearly identified product, enter the sales category in the sales order line and leave the item number field empty.

side effect of this rework is that every reference to entities that are now shared must be updated to reference the new tables.

Technical

In Microsoft Dynamics AX 2009, all items were stored in a single table (InventTable). There were three item types available: Service, BOM (bill of materials), and Item. Each item was associated with a mandatory dimension group, item group, and item model group. All possible item combinations were stored in a single table (InventDimCombination). All item creations and setup processes were stored within a company account context, and the virtual table collection approach was used to share the item master data within different company accounts.

In Microsoft Dynamics AX 2012 all product master data is shared across all companies, and the virtual table collection concept is no longer available for product master data management. The old item representation (InventTable) still exists. However, it now has a foreign key to the shared product instance (EcoResProduct hierarchy), and it represents the released product concept or a given enterprise product that has become authorized for use within a legal entity. In addition, products can now only be a service type product or an item type product.

BOM has been removed as an item type, though an Item type product can still have a BOM associated with it. The new default order-type policy on the legal-entity level defines whether the BOM structure will be used and whether a production order should be created to fulfill the demand. You can set the order type to 'purchase' and associate a BOM with it if the product type is set to 'item'.

The inventory dimension group has been split and refactored into three groups: product dimension, storage dimension, and tracking dimension. These groups can be associated with the shared product entity or overridden at the legal-entity level. The old item combinations representation (InventDimCombination) still exists, but it now has a foreign key to the shared product variant entity (EcoResDistinctProductVariant table) and represents a released product variant or a given shared product variant that is authorized for use within a legal entity. All products have the enterprise data definition set up like translation data. First, the product entity must be created on the enterprise or system level. Then the product must be released to a given legal entity, and all company-specific master data must be specified before the released product can be authorized for use for certain processes.

The item group and item model group are still defined on legal-entity level; however, the relationship between entities and the old item entity has been refactored completely.

In previous versions, all inventory items and services were company-specific and were stored in the InventTable. Items could vary in system-predefined item dimensions (size, color, and configuration). The system used the concept of item combinations to associate an ItemId with item dimensions. All item and item-combinations master data were stored in a company context.

The virtual table collection approach was the recommended way to share item master data across companies, if needed.

In Microsoft Dynamics AX 2012 **all** products are stored as system master data, which allows organizations to create and maintain shared product definition data.

The product master concept means the product definition, which can have variants in product dimensions (color, size, and configuration).

The product variant concept means a product that has a number of associated product dimension values (color, size, and configuration). It replaces the previous item combination concept. It is important to note that a product variant has all attributes and behaviors that any other type of product has.

The distinct product concept means a product that does not vary in product dimensions and therefore cannot have a product dimension group associated to it.

The products in a system can be released to a legal entity to become available for various processes (sales, purchase, and production). The same shared product variants can be available for production in one company, but not available for the production in another legal entity.

Product dimension values like colors, sizes, and configuration are stored in the system tables (EcoResColor, EcoResConfiguration, and EcoResSize) and are immutable. The InventDim product dimensions values point to the EcoResColor.Name, EcoResConfiguration.Name, and EcoResSize.Name fields.

To allow for a more centralized process across legal entities, Microsoft Dynamics AX 2012 introduces the concept of products, or more exactly, product definitions. Product definitions are created independently of a legal entity. Therefore, core values such as product number, type, and name are shared. Some core values can be overridden by a legal entity, such as the search name, whereas other values are kept as key definition attributes and therefore cannot be changed other than on the actual product definition. The product information management process involves several terms and concepts which will be explained below.

A product is a uniquely identifiable product. It serves as a core product that does not vary. Therefore, no product dimensions can be associated with the definition.

A product master is a standard or functional product representation that is the basis for configuring product variants. The variations are configured by selecting a configuration technology. This can be either a set of predefined product dimensions or by using product configurations in sales scenarios.

A product variant represents the configuration of a product master. Based on the choice of the configuration technology, the variant can be either predefined by using the product dimensions of its master or configured by using a configurator tool.

Product Information Management

A product in Microsoft Dynamics AX 2012 consists of a core product definition.

This is defined independent of the organization where it is used. When the product is authorized for use in a legal entity, the additional organizationally dependent details, such as costing, coverage plans, taxation information, and preferred vendors for supplying the product and much more, are set up in the respective legal entities.

The authorization process is supported by a product release function. This enables users to select products that include variations and make them available in one or more legal entities.

From a decentralized process, products can be created and maintained directly from the Released products list page in the Product information management module, given the user has the security role to follow these steps. These duties are included in the Product designer and Product design manager roles. By enabling these tasks, the system makes sure that upon product creation in a legal entity, a core product definition is automatically released back to the enterprise products repository.

Product types

The following are two types of products that can be defined manually in Microsoft Dynamics AX 2012:

- Products - these are clearly identifiable products that do not have variations associated with them. You can think of them as standard or base products. User interface provides the Products list page in the Product information management module to view and manage products.

- Product masters - these serve as templates or models for variants. The variants of a product master can be either predefined or created in sales scenarios by using a product configurator. A product master is associated with one or more product dimensions, or for some configurators, product attributes. Use the Product masters list page in the Product information management module to view and manage product masters

Another option is to view all products and product masters in the All products and product masters list page (Product information management > Common > Products > All products and product masters).

Product creation process

Creating a new product involves the following four-step process:

1. Create and define the product.
2. Release it to legal entities.
3. Define legal entity specific data.
4. Use the released product in specific legal entity.

When you create a new product definition, the type and sub-type are the key attributes to enter. They determine the additional functions and required setup.

The product type classifies whether a product is tangible[6] or intangible[7] (item or service), whereas the sub-type is a sub-classification of the product.

Product identification – the product identifier is defined at enterprise level, together with the product name. When releasing the product to a company, the released product inherits the same number as the enterprise product (but can be optionally overridden).

Product description is defined at enterprise level and is inherited for the released product. Optional language translations are available (see the Product translation section below).

---

[6] Something is considered a good if it is a tangible item. That is, it is something that is felt, tasted, heard, smelled or seen. For example, bicycles, cell phones, and donuts are all examples of tangible goods.

[7] Something is considered a service if it is an offering a customer obtains through the work or labor of someone else. Services can result in the creation of tangible goods (e.g., a publisher of business magazines hires a freelance writer to write an article) but the main solution being purchased is the service. Unlike goods, services are not stored, they are only available at the time of use (e.g., hair salon) and the consistency of the benefit offered can vary from one purchaser to another (e.g., not exactly the same hair styling each time).

Technical

In Microsoft Dynamics AX 2009, ItemId was the main item identification value. A common pattern was to add a relation to InventTable by the ItemId field in order to model a relationship to the item master; and then to add the InventDimID field to the table to represent an item master (in case InventDimID was a blank value) or a given item combination; and finally to specify additional storage dimensions, which were controlled by the item dimension group setup. There was no single way to ensure that the same items in the different companies were equal. The best practice was to reuse the same ItemId values or to use virtual table collections to share the item master data across companies.

In Microsoft Dynamics AX 2012, product is identified by a unique shared product number value, which is a natural key of the product entity. Not all types of products can have a unique product number. The product variants do not have their own shared product number since they are always identified by the relation to their product master.

Product Translation

The product translations are mainly used for output on external documents, whereas the data values will always be shown in the system language, for example, when you open and view the product related list pages and forms.

On external documents, the product name will be displayed according to the company language or the preferred language by the customer or vendor.

In previous versions, the system allowed the user to specify descriptions for items and item combinations in different languages but there could be only one Name specified for an item or an item combination in the company-specific language.

In Microsoft Dynamics AX 2012, the system allows users to define multi-language translations for shared product definitions. Out of the box, the product localization attributes are the product name and the product description. Product search name has been introduced in order to control shared and legal-entity–specific values to the product —alias functionality.

By default, the product has its name and translation in the system language (enterprise organizational language).

The pattern that is applied to model product localization is consistent across the application to model localization support for shared entities. The general system translation forms are used to manage product translation, which enables a consistent user experience in the way that the user interacts with the various entities in the system regarding multi-language translation (product, attributes, catalog descriptions, and so on).

The Text translation form enables you to have product translations. You can enter descriptions and product names for multiple languages. However, the product name and description are optional; only the product number is required.

Variant configuration

In Microsoft Dynamics AX 2009, the item master contained a number of fields that were used for various features to create new item combinations. This included features like Product Builder and Standard Configurator. In addition, the item master contained fields that directly affect the creation of new item combinations.

In Microsoft Dynamics AX 2012, the product master contains a mandatory policy that identifies the process of its variant creation. This shared policy is called variant configuration technology. This setup identifies the only possible feature that can be used to create related product variants. The Microsoft Dynamics AX 2009 code base is adjusted and modified to follow the product master setup, so any modification in this area should be adjusted as well.

Product, Storage, and Tracking dimension groups

In Microsoft Dynamics AX 2009, the item dimension group was a mandatory item master setting. You could not create an item without specifying a dimension group (mandatory field at item creation), and each item always had to have one - and only one - dimension group associated to it. The dimension group was company-specific and was logically grouped around item dimensions and storage dimensions. The virtual table collection approach was the recommended way to share dimensions groups across companies, if necessary.

In Microsoft Dynamics AX 2012 the item dimension group is split into three groups: the product dimension group, storage dimension group, and tracking dimension group. These are the shared entities. They are assigned to the system product definition and can be assigned to the legal-entity level as well. In other words, you can define how your product should behave in a centralized way (always controlled by serial number) or you can define legal-entity–specific behavior. Note that the dimensions group setup has been changed in order to ensure better consistency.

Product dimension groups

In Microsoft Dynamics AX 2009, item master dimensions (color, size, and configuration) were stored in company-specific tables and could not be shared across multiple companies. When the item or item combination was selected on the order line, the InventDim structure held relationships to the company-specific item dimensions.

The system allowed lookup of company-specific item dimensions on the order line and always validated them against existing item combinations.

The item master contained default dimensions, which could be set and used as the default user choice during journal line creation.

In Microsoft Dynamics AX 2012 product dimensions are shared and are attribute-based. Three predefined attributes exist, representing color, size, and configuration dimensions.

Technical

The product dimension values are stored in a shared, immutable table (EcoResColor, EcoResSize, and EcoResConfiguration). The database schema around product dimensions allows adding new attributes, which can be used to represent new product dimensions. For example, you could have T-shirt sizes (X, L, M) and shoe sizes (8, 10, 12).

The product master holds relations to all possible product dimensions values within one product attribute. The product variant holds one and only one relation to the product dimensions value within one product attribute.

The InventDim structure holds the relationships to the shared product dimension values.

The system allows lookup only of legal-entity–specific product dimensions on the order line and always validates them against release product variants for the current legal entity. On the shared level (product management forms, tables, and so on), the system allows lookup of all product dimensions and validates them again all product variants.

As a clear difference to product attributes, product dimensions let you track their values in all major processes, such as for cost, inventory, and analysis purposes.

Whereas product attributes can be associated with products and product masters, product dimensions can only be used together with product masters (except for masters that are configured by using the option constraint-based configuration).

This is because they make up the uniqueness of a product master's variations.

You can determine which product dimensions are mandatory for a given product master by selecting the appropriate product dimension group when you create the product master.

The product dimension group is set up from Product information management > Setup > Dimension groups > Product dimension groups.

Color and size product dimensions are provided out of the box. However, if the dimension labels do not make sense in your organization, those two can be renamed. The only exception is the Configuration product dimension, that cannot be renamed.

Because the product dimensions provide the uniqueness of a variation, the following rules apply:

- The dimension must be specified when product transactions are created, for example when a purchase or sales order line is created.

- The specified dimension applies only to the product transaction. You can neither fully nor partly change the dimension value for the related inventory transactions upon physical issue or receipt.

- Products are always reserved for each dimension. You cannot reserve products for dimension values other than those specified on the action product transaction.

Storage dimension groups

Another important information needed in an ERP is how the product is stored and drawn from inventory and enable inventory to be managed on a detailed level. When we say storage dimensions we mean site, warehouse, location, and pallet ID information that and can be allocated to products only when the product's stocking dimension group allows for it. A storage dimension determines where and how a product is stored.

A site is an area of ground on which a building or group of buildings is constructed, but multiple application can be found for this storage dimension, such as the financial analysis on inventory.

A warehouse is a storage location, such as a building.

A location is a detailed item storage location, specifying on which aisle-rack-shelf-bin the item is found. Typically, this dimension is used when you operate with Warehouse management.

A Pallet ID represent an identification for a group of products on the same pallet. Use only when operating with Warehouse management.

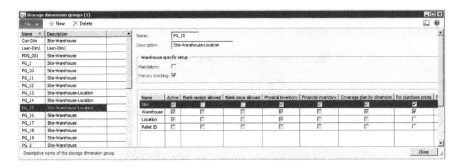

Tracking dimension groups

The tracking dimension group concerns the traceability of the inventory in the system. Traceability is useful for quality assurance purposes and when you deal with warranties for a product. The tracing functionality is especially important for products that represent a certain risk or are under strict control (by government, for example), such as medicine or chemicals, where defects in production could lead to the product's recall. It is equally important for guaranteed items to be able to trace back to the date that the product was manufactured or sold. Serial and batch numbers allow for this kind of functionality.

You can assign serial numbers, batch numbers, or both to an inventory product. Serial numbers are assigned to individual items, and batch numbers are assigned to a set of products.

Some commonly misunderstanding regarding traceability is caused by AX terminology and occur around system reserved word Lot ID. Because most of the customers desire lot-tracing, this can create confusion. Lot ID is the term that refers to a transaction, and not a product dimension such as serial and batch numbers. A Lot ID is assigned automatically to each sales or purchase line when you create it. The number is taken from the number sequence that is associated with the number sequence reference Lot No. in the inventory parameters. You cannot make transactions without a Lot ID being assigned, unlike when you use batch numbers that you can either select to use or not.

All products must be assigned a tracking dimension group. If you do not want the tracking group to track the product, do not select the Active check box on the batch number and serial number.

To define that the dimension does not have to be specified when physical receipts are updated select the Blank receipt allow check box. This functionality is useful if, for example, you do not want to specify the serial/batch number upon input but you do for picking and output (for example, you track your sold products with your own tracking codes instead of using vendor's serial/batch number).

To define that the dimension does not have to be specified when physical issues are updated, select the Blank issue allow check box.

For example, when a product is traced for quality assurance reasons, the item tracing functionality is very usefull. Let's say that a problem is found with a batch of sugar. The Quality Manager wants to perform an item trace for the batch. He opens the **Item tracing** form (see below) and performs a trace for that batch of sugar.

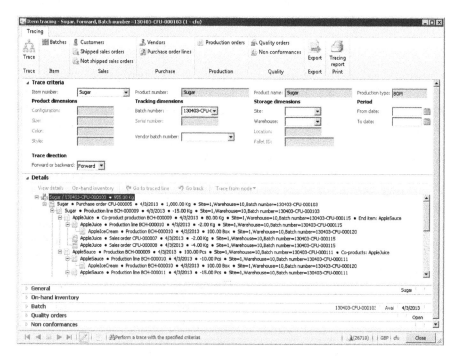

Item group

Item group is the product classification for inventory items, and it is the integration point between the inventory and financial module.

In Microsoft Dynamics AX 2009, the item group was a mandatory item master setting. You could not create an item without specifying the item group, and every item always had to have one—and only one—item group associated with it. The item group was company-specific and contained important account setup for purchase, inventory, and sales processes. The virtual table collection approach was a recommended way to share these settings across companies, if necessary.

In Microsoft Dynamics AX 2012, the item group is not mandatory for the product at enterprise level, but it is still company-specific mandatory. In other words, you can create the instance of a released product without specifying the item group at the creation step or at the product release step. The item group can be assigned later to the product when needed (or by applying a product template).

The product can be used for certain processes without having these values set up (for example, trade agreement setup). If a process expects an item group to be set up (for example, sales-order line creation), a run-time error will occur, and the user will be prompted to set the value on the product before continuing his or her action.

Item model group

In Item model group we find the main configuration and setup of inventory costing in Microsoft Dynamics AX, where we identify the inventory costing valuation method, but we can also setup the desired behavior for warehouse management and operations. For inventory model group, navigate to Inventory and warehouse management > Setup > Inventory > Item model group. Microsoft Dynamics AX 2012 supports the following inventory valuation methods: FIFO, LIFO, LIFO Date, Weighted Average, Weighted Average Date, Standard Cost and Moving Average.

In Microsoft Dynamics AX 2009, the item model group was a mandatory item master setting also. You could not create an item without specifying the item model group, and each item always had to have one and only one item model group associated with it. The item model group was company-specific and contained important setup information about the inventory model and warehouse management settings. The virtual table collection approach was a recommended way to share these settings across companies, if necessary.

In Microsoft Dynamics AX 2012, the item model group is not mandatory for the product at enterprise level, but it is still company-specific mandatory. In other words, you can create the instance of a released product without specifying the item model group at the creation step or at the product-release step. The item model group can be assigned later to the product when needed (or by applying a product template).

The product can be used for certain processes without having these values set (for example, trade agreement setup). If a process expects an item model group to be set up (for example, sales order line creation), a run-time error will occur and the user will be prompted to set the value on the product before continuing his or her action.

Products

As in Microsoft Dynamics AX 2009, the product type classifies whether a product is tangible or intangible (an item or a service). In Microsoft Dynamics AX 2012, this distinction is made as a subclassification of the product.

There are three subtypes of products: product master, distinct product, and product variant. Product variants will be variants of product masters.

This concept is designed as a super-type/subtype table hierarchy to decouple specific properties between different entities that are of the same nature.

A product master is associated to the EcoResProductDimensionGroup and can have a range of predefined product dimensions available. For example, a T-shirt could be a product master with various sizes (S, M, L) and colors (Blue, Green). The product variant represents variations of the product master.

Technical

In Microsoft Dynamics AX 2009, a special value of ItemType::BOM could be associated to an item. This itemType meant that the item could have a BOM and route associated with it. In other words, the item master had to be of BOM type in order to have a Bill of Materials and to be produced. An item master whose type was set to Item normally would represent only items designated for purchase.

In Microsoft Dynamics AX 2012, the ItemType::BOM value has been removed. The value that represents items that can be manufactured or purchased is now itemType::Item. A new mandatory default order setting has been introduced to indicate when an item must be purchased or manufactured by default. This policy is stored in the InventItemSetupSupplyType table.

By contrast, a distinct product cannot have variations (that is, it cannot have any product dimensions specified).

Product templates

If there are many similarities between the setups of multiple legal entity products, it is recommended that you use a product template. Product templates are used to copy information from a released product to other selected released products or to apply the same information to an already configured product. Product templates help streamline the process for setting up legal entity specific data for products when there are many values that are the same from one product to another. There are two types of templates that can be created: personal templates and shared templates. A personal template is available only by the user who created the template, whereas a shared template can be accessed by any user in the system.

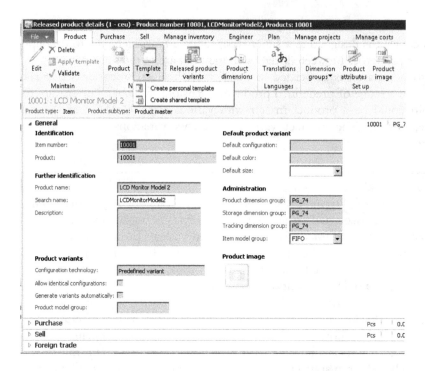

User can apply a template to existing products, by selecting one or multiple products and clicking Apply template button on the Product action pane.

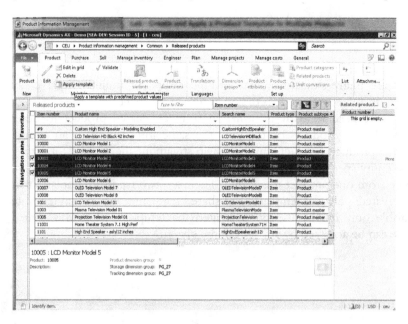

Category Hierarchies and Categories

Category hierarchies are used to classify products, vendors, customers or transactions for reporting and analysis purposes. Each category hierarchy consists of a structure of subcategories. An organization can create more than one category hierarchy. For example, your organization might create one category hierarchy for classifying purchased products and another hierarchy for classifying vendors.

The number of category hierarchies used by your organization, and the structure and number of codes for each category hierarchy depend on the following:

- Processes of the organization
- The products and services purchased or sold
- The industry standards that apply
- The reporting requirements for the organization

Product categories available in the sales process belong to the sales category hierarchy. An important category setting for sales process is the sales tax group, which may be entered in the Item sales tax groups tab of the sales categories (Sales and marketing->Setup->Categories->Sales categories).

Categorize Products

Product categories can be assigned to products that are used for building procurement catalogs. This step is required before a product can be added to a procurement catalog.

Define Product Attributes

Product attributes identify the details that you want to maintain for your products such as Stock-keeping unit (SKU) number, product version, and so on, and provide additional details that your organization might want to record for a particular product or category. You can associate product attributes together with a product through the category to which the product belongs. When you add a category and its associated products to your procurement catalog, the attributes assigned to the procurement category are imported into the catalog and can be displayed on the procurement site.

When you define product attributes, you must first define the attribute type and then assign the attribute type to the attribute. The attribute type identifies the type of data that can be entered for a specific attribute and a list or range of valid values that can be used for the attribute. The attribute is the value that is displayed with the product to provide the requester additional details about the product.

Note: Depending on the attribute type that you select, the Default value field might be displayed as a check box, a drop-down field, or it might have additional required data such as a unit of measure or currency.

After you create attribute types and product attributes, you must assign the product attributes to categories. Next you must assign the category to the product, and then you can define values for the product attributes.

Order quantity modifiers

The product's standard sales order quantity and the default sales unit of measure act as default values when you enter a sales order line item. The system provides a soft warning if the entered quantity does not comply with the product's order quantity modifiers of minimum, maximum, and multiple.

Product sales price

A product's sales price can be predefined in several different ways. The basic approaches include a standard sales price that can be manually specified or automatically calculated. Additional approaches to a product's sales price will be covered in the context of sales order and sales quotation, such as the use of sales price trade agreements and sales agreements.

As the simplest approach, a product's standard sales price can be defined in terms of its default sales unit of measure. It represents a company-wide sales price that acts as the default on a sales line when other sources of pricing information do not exist. This standard sales price can be manually specified or calculated, and the calculations differ for a purchased product versus a manufactured product.

With a purchased product, the product's standard purchase price and a specified markup percentage (or contribution ratio) can be used to calculate its standard sales price. This is continuously recalculated based on changes to the product's standard purchase price as the result of the last vendor invoice.

With a manufactured product, the standard sales price can be updated by activating a product's sales price record, where the sales price is calculated based on a cost-plus-markup approach for its purchased components, routing operations, and overhead formulas.

Unit of measure

In Microsoft Dynamics AX 2012, a product cannot be sold or purchased unless a unit of measure is associated with it. You must specify all units that a company uses in the Units form.

In the Released products form, you can specify units of measure for purchase orders, inventory, and sales orders. For example, a product might be purchased in pounds, stocked in liters, and sold in pints.

Catch Weight Items

Catch weight items are commonly used for food products involving protein or for agricultural produce. They are also used in other industries, such as metals, mining, and paper. A catch weight item is characterized by two units of measure – weight/volume/area and pieces – for the purpose of reporting inventory transactions and viewing inventory balances.

Weight/volume/area represents the item's inventory unit of measure, such as pounds or kilograms, although some industries might use volume or area instead (for example, square inches). This is the unit of measure at which the item is billed or invoiced.

Pieces represent the item's catch weight unit of measure, where you define the average weight per piece (also known as the nominal weight), and inventory transactions are ported in pieces and their actual weight. Examples of pieces include a 10-pound box, 100-pound package, 2,500-pound tote, 5-kilogram bag, 50-pound case, 200-kilogram crate, 275-gallon tote, 330-gallon tote, 8-GA 48×48 sheet, or some other unit of measure with zero decimal places (that is, 0 decimal precision). The catch weight unit is considered a "handling" unit of measure.

The multiple units of measure for a catch weight item should not be confused with a fixed unit of measure conversion factor (sometimes called a dual unit of measure), because each piece of a catch weight can have a different actual weight within the range defined for the item.

The allowable variation in the weight per catch weight piece should be defined in such a way that customers who receive a product with the total weight at either end of the range will not be disappointed or have their expectations unmet. For example, a turkey might vary from as few as 6 pounds to as much as 28 pounds. However, a customer who wanted three turkeys might not be happy to receive three turkeys at just 6 pounds each. Therefore, the turkeys might be defined as four different items: small turkeys weighing between 6 and 9 pounds, medium turkeys weighing between 9.1 and 13 pounds, medium-large turkeys weighing between 13.1 and 18 pounds, and large turkeys weighing between 18.1 and 28 pounds. Each of these items would be defined with an average or nominal weight.

As shown in the preceding example, transactions are driven by the catch weight quantity. Sales orders, purchase orders, transfer orders, and production orders specify how many pieces of the catch weight item are needed. However, the actual weight of each piece is recorded, and the pricing is done according to that actual weight, not the number of pieces.

A catch weight item is a stocked item that might be purchased or manufactured. Catch weight items do not require the batch number dimension, because batch numbers are optional, depending on the industry.

The serial number dimension is required in some definitions of catch weight items. The catch weight item is defined in Microsoft Dynamics AX 2012 at the global enterprise level. An item cannot be a catch weight item in one company and a non-catch weight item in another company.

The catch weight items related sales process will be similar to the normal items sales process, except the CW quantity field that needs to be managed at all levels.

4 SALES QUOTATIONS

A sales quotation is a source document that is used to document an offer to supply a quantity of product for a specified price and by a specified date in response to a request for quotation in a sales process.

Issuing a quotation resembles the process for issuing a sales order. Most functionality found in the Sales order form is also available in the Sales quotation form.

Sometimes, your customers want more than one quotation for the items that they are interested in. Typically, they want items in a range of prices. In these situations, you can send several alternative quotations and link them. Each quotation might reflect different materials (for example, steel, copper, or aluminum) or different finishes (for example, brushed, polished, or matte). Quotations accepted by customers are converted to sales orders, while alternative quotations are lost with the possibility of attaching a reason code for losing it.

Sales Quotation Business Use
You can use sales quotations to:

- Issue sales quotations to customers or prospects[8]; a mandatory step when issuing a sales order from a sales quotation to a prospect is the conversion of the prospect into a customer;
- Update sales quotations; a sales quotation can be updated and the system will save different versions of quotations for future references;
- Convert sales quotations to sales orders;

---

[8] Prospects are companies or persons which are not customers yet.

- Create sales quotation templates; using Word templates enables standard formatted quotations that contains information from the system;
- Mass create, update, and delete sales quotations;
- Copy sales quotations, thus boosting productivity for similar quotation processing;
- Apply trade agreements, supplementary items, and charges to sales quotations;
- Use enhanced delivery date features;
- View the Bill of Material (BOM) for sales quotation line items and make updates to the BOM;
- Include sales quotation items in master scheduling (please see the Application specification box below).

Before you start to work with sales quotations, you must make some quotation related settings like number sequences, default values and so on. When a new quotation is created, the system will take the ID from the Quotation number series. Sending a quotation to the prospect/customer will also use a number sequence termed Quotation journal, while confirming a quotation will populate the Quotation Confirmation field with a number from the Quotation Confirmation number sequence.

Application

Microsoft recommends that you obtain a full Microsoft Dynamics CRM license. If you do not have a CRM license, all quotations are included in the master plan, regardless of the probability that they will be converted to actual orders. Including all quotations in the master plan could lead to an unnecessary increase of inventory if the quotations are not confirmed.

If you have a CRM license, you can include only quotations that have a high probability of being converted to orders. For example, if you enter a probability percentage of 85, all quotations that have a probability of 85 percent and more are included.

You may find it useful to include only quotations that have a high probability of conversion to orders if you want to have items in stock so that you can deliver them at the time that is promised in the quotation.

Setup Tables

In addition to the number sequences, there are several setup tables for sales quotations. Like all other setup tables, the values in these tables should reflect and support the company's business processes.

The setup tables include the following:

- Types: Indicate the kind of sale the quotation is. They can be used for statistics for sales management because they help track and analyze the sales quotations. Examples can include Campaign, New sale, and One time.

- Template groups: Create groups for quotation templates. For example, a company can have a special event (Easter) sale. As part of the sale, there can be three templates with different product offerings. Use template groups to group all three templates as part of the Easter sale.

- Document titles: Create-commonly used or generic titles for quotation documents. For example, a specific title used for all Autumn offers. These titles are printed on quotation documents.

- Document introductions: Create and store common salutations and introductions to quotation documents. These introductions are printed on quotation documents.

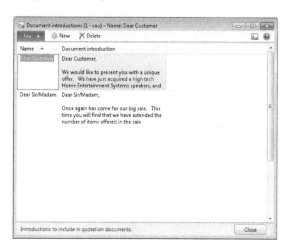

- Document conclusions: Create and maintain standard concluding sentences or paragraphs for quotation documents. These conclusions are printed on quotation documents.

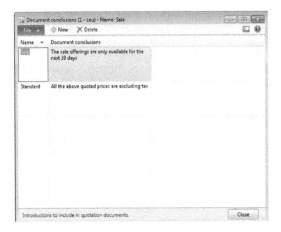

Default Values

You can set up quotation default values in the Sales FastTab on the General tab of the Accounts receivable parameters form in the Accounts receivable module.

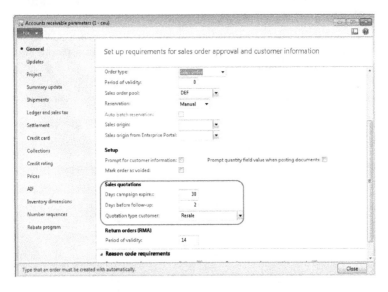

You can set up the default values in the following fields:

- Days campaign expires: Enter the number of days for the quotation expiration date. When you create a quotation, the expiration date of the quotation is automatically calculated as today's date plus the number of days specified in this field.

- Days before follow up: Enter the number of days for the quotation follow-up date. When you create a quotation, the follow-up date of the associated activity is automatically calculated as today's date plus the number of days specified in this field.
- Quotation type customer: This field refers to the Type setup table explained earlier. The type of quotation can default when a sales quotation is created.

Working with Quotations

One of the main activities as a salesperson is to maintain quotations for your customers. He can create sales quotations upon customer requests and in mass by using quotation templates. He can change quotations and reprint them or he can enter alternative quotations that will be managed simultaneous, and even make price simulations for each quotation line. It is also salesperson's responsibility to follow up on the status of his sales quotations: those that are canceled, lost and won.

Creating Sales Quotations

Creating a quotation resembles creating a sales order:

- Several different list pages help sort and view existing quotations, from which you can create a quotation. The list pages can display all quotations, open quotations, user quotations (My quotations), expiring quotations, sent quotations, etc.
- Create header information about the quotation in the Header view of the Sales quotation form.
- Create the individual lines in the Line view of the Sales quotation form. Create quotations from the Sales and marketing module and the Enterprise Portal.

To create a sales quotation from the Sales and marketing module, follow the path Sales and marketing > Common Forms > Sales quotation > All Quotations, click Sales quotation in the New group of the Action Pane and then the Create quotation form opens.

Note: It is possible to create a new quotation from an opportunity. The usual scenario is that a sales representative calls a customer for a follow up on an existing opportunity and the customer may request a quotation.

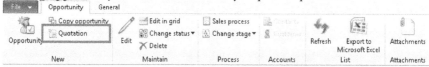

Note: Another option is to create a new Project quotation, with a reference to a project ID. Use this option when the company's activity is tracked by projects.

The Type, Expiration date, and Follow-up date fields default according to the default values that are set up.

As mentioned earlier, the Account type for which the quotation will be created can be Customer or Prospect. Depending of the account type selected, the system selects Customer account or Prospect drop-down list appropriately. This action transfers the prospect and customer values to the quotation header. This includes the price discount groups associated with the account.

Click OK to close the Create quotation form and the new quotation is opened in Edit mode. To add the quotation details (lines) click Add line to create a new line on the Lines tab of the Sales quotation form. Lines can be products or sales categories, if the product on the sales quotation does not have an item number.

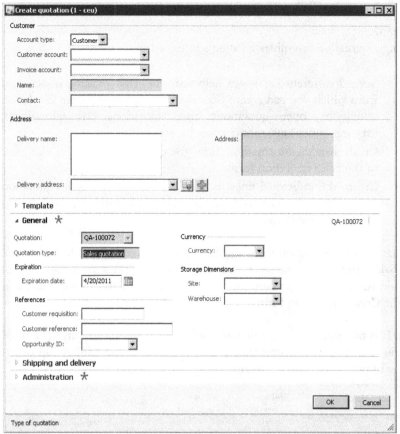

Selecting a product searches the system for a valid combination of sales price and line discounts that are part of any trade agreements that apply to the selected item and customer. Any applicable price and line discounts are applied to the line item. When all lines are entered, quotation can be send to customer.

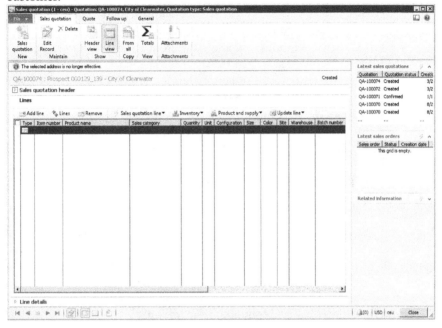

Updating Sales Quotations

Each sales quotation has a quotation status. The quotation status does not refer to a particular quotation status setup table. The status values are fixed in the system.

The status is changed by various processes in the quotation. The quotation statuses are as follows:

- Created: When the sales quotation is originally generated, the status is set to created.
- Sent: The Quotation is generated. On the Sales quotation form, from the Quotation tab in the Action Pane, click Send quotation in the Generate group. This opens the Send quotation form, where you can generate a printed quotation.

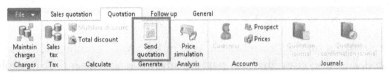

- Confirmed: The quotation is confirmed and converted to a sales order. The confirmation date is inserted into the quotation and the quotation is closed for editing. From the Follow up tab in the Action Pane, click Confirm in the Status group. This opens the Confirm quotation form.

- Lost: The quotation is lost and a different company won the quote. From the Follow up tab in the Action Pane, click Lost in the Status group. This opens the Lose quotation form, and when it is complete updates the status to lost and is closed for editing.

- Canceled: The quotation is canceled because the customer no longer needs the goods requested. From the Follow up tab in the Action Pane, click Cancel in the Status group. This opens the Cancel quotation form, and when it is complete updates the status to canceled and is closed for editing.

Confirm a Sales Quotation

When the sales quotation is confirmed, the system ask for a reason why the quotation was confirmed (for example, price) and then creates a sales order, copies all values from the sales quotation to the sales order, creates a quotation confirmation journal record, inserts the confirmation date into the sales quotation as the current system date, sets the Quotation status to Confirmed and closes the sales quotation for editing.

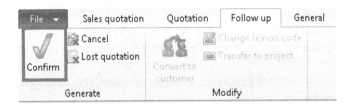

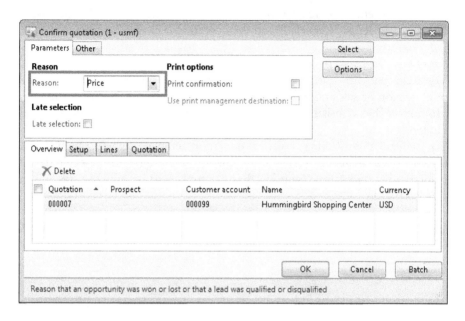

The new sales order is shown in the Latest sales orders section on fact box on the right-hand side (the Latest sales orders fact box might need to be expanded). The user can click on the sales order number to view the sales order and the sales order line details.

Lose a Sales Quotation

To set the status of a sales quotation to Lost, in the Follow up tab in the Action Pane, you can click Lost Quotation in the Status group. You are then prompted to enter the reason the sales quotation is lost. The Quotation status is then set to "Lost" and the quotation is closed for editing.

Cancel a Sales Quotation

To set the status of a sales quotation to Canceled, you can click Cancel in the Status group on the Follow up tab in the Action Pane. You are then prompted to enter the reason the sales quotation is canceled. The Quotation status is then set to "Canceled" and the quotation is closed for editing.

Sales Quotation Template

You can set up quotation templates to ease the mass creation and modification of sales quotations. For example, a company can offer a holiday promotion that consists of three offerings, each with different items to be quoted.

To facilitate this offering, create a quotation template, which can be done starting from an existing sales quotation on which you can specify that it belongs to a template Group ID, has a template name and has the Active checkmark On.

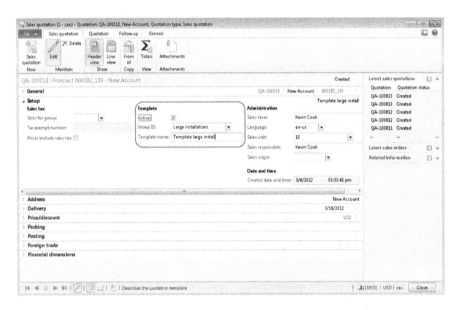

Next time user wants to create a new sales quotation and wants to apply a template he can select an active template on the Create quotation form. Also, by selecting a Calculation Method, the user decides if item prices are based on the standard hierarchy for finding prices and discounts, such as product sales price, and trade agreements (Based on current values) or all information that is not customer specific, such as dimensions and item prices, is taken from the template (Based on template values).

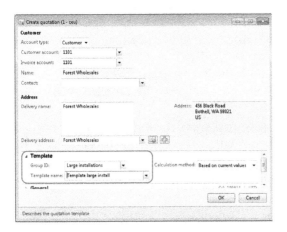

Note: Only active templates can be used when you apply a template to a new sales quotation.

Mass Creation of Sales Quotations

If you have to create similar quotations for many different sales targets, you can mass create the quotations instead of creating them one-by-one. You can do this for sales quotations and project quotations. When you mass create any kind of quotation, you must base the quotation on a quotation template. To mass create sales quotations, you have to access the Periodic job Mass create quotations, specify the account type, specify the template group and template name and the calculation method. By using the Select button you can specify additional criteria for the mass sales quotation creation.

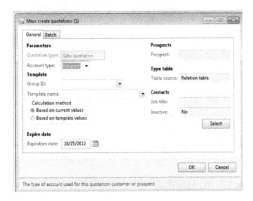

If no contacts are selected or filtered, sales quotations for the customer or prospect are sent to all contacts who are associated with this customer or prospect. If no contacts are associated with the customer or prospect, no sales quotations are created.

Other Sales Quotations Periodic Updates

Many sales quotations can be updated at the same time. The options for mass update are found in the Sales and marketing > Periodic > Quotation update folder.

The options for mass updates include the following:

- Cancel quotation: All sales quotations can be canceled at the same time.
- Lose quotation: All sales quotations can be lost at the same time.
- Mass create quotation: All sales quotations can be created at the same time.
- Confirm quotation: All sales quotations can be confirmed at the same time.
- Sent quotation: All sales quotations can be printed at the same time.

Printing Sales Quotations

If sales quotation information changes, it can be reprinted by clicking Send quotation in the Generate group on the Quote tab in the Action Pane. This not only activates the quotation to be reprinted but creates a new Quotation journal record also.

The salesperson creates the sales quotation, prints it, and mails it to the customer. After they receive the quotation, the customer contacts the salesperson and changes the quantity of products. The salesperson updates the sales quotation and generates the quotation. This not only prints the sales quotation, it creates another contractual offer by the company which is recorded as a new sales quotation journal.

Only the most recent quotation is used when confirming to a sales order.

The quotation journal records are accessed by following the path Sales and marketing > Inquiries > Journals > Quotation.

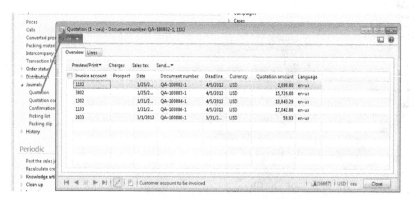

Deleting Sales Quotations

There are two methods to delete a sales quotation, either delete sales quotation records individually or by marking records, either delete sales quotation records in mass by using the Delete quotations form. Only sales quotations with a status of Created, Confirmed, Lost, or Canceled can be deleted.

Additional Sales Quotation Features

The following features are available for sales quotations:

- Copy from all
- Manage competitors
- Trade agreements and supplementary items
- Enhanced delivery date features
- Charges
- Working with BOMs
- Multiple ship to addresses
- Quotations included in Master scheduling
- Price simulation

Copy From All

You can use the Copy from all feature to save time and prevent sales quotation information from being entered from scratch, and to copy the whole quotation or specific pieces of different quotations.

The Copy from all feature copies the same information as in sales orders. However, the information is only from other sales quotations. You can access the From all button in the Copy group on the Action Pane from the Sales quotation form.

The Copy from all form displays a list of sales quotations. You can select the sales quotation or the sales quotation line items to copy. If you click Select all on the quotation line all the sales quotation lines underneath are copied to the new sales quotation. If you do not want to select the quotation lines, manually select the Mark check box on the appropriate quotation line(s).

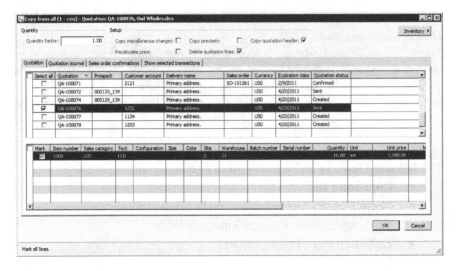

Manage competitors

You can add competitors to a quotation and this can provide a further analysis about the result of competing against them, for example indicating quotations won.

Trade Agreements and Supplementary Items

You can use trade agreements to set up discounts and prices for sales orders and sales quotations. Trade agreement options include the following:

- Sales price: The customer receives special pricing for certain items.
- Line discount: The customer receives a discount if the quantity on a sales quotation line meets the minimum quantity required by the agreement.
- Multiline discount: This discount works the same as the Line discount with one difference: the customer receives a discount if the quantity on all the applicable lines in a sales quotation meets the minimum quantity required by the agreement.
- Total discount: The customer receives a discount on the whole quotation.

You can access the trade agreement functionality from the General tab in the Action Pane, by clicking the Trade agreement button in the Customer group.
Another option that you can access from the General tab is the Supplementary sales items that are set up for items in relation to the customer on the sales quotation. This option can also be found from the sales quotation line by clicking Sales quotation line > Supplementary items from the Action Pane. This functionality works the same as it does for sales orders.

Trade agreements within Microsoft Dynamics AX 2012 provide high flexibility and granularity for controlling sales prices and discounts. The trade agreement types include price, line discount, multiline discount, and total discount and can be specified for a large range of trade agreement conditions (customer/segment of customers, item/segment of items, product dimensions, storage dimensions, tracking dimensions, price break, unit of measure, currency, and effective dates).

Microsoft Dynamics AX 2012 supports a large variety of functionality that provides overview and transparency and that simplifies maintenance and reduces the resources needed to manage the trade agreements:

- Select – Extracting active trade agreements into the trade agreement journal is simple and precise.
- Smart rounding – This feature supports psychological pricing by controlling price endings per price interval and currency.
- Copy and revise – New trade agreements can be created manually or by copying and modifying existing trade agreements in one process step. (This includes the option to copy and convert purchase prices into sales prices.)
- Bulk editing – You can bulk update trade agreements when common changes apply. Use smart rounding after bulk editing to ensure price endings for sales prices.
- Generic currency – Sales prices can be maintained in one currency and automatically converted to any other currency at the time of order taking. Dedicated exchange rates are used solely for sales prices, with their own rates and update frequency. Use smart rounding after conversion to ensure price endings for sales prices.
- Segregation of duties – The security framework lets you divide the maintenance task into two required operations: entering trade agreements by the clerk, and approval and activation by the manager.
- Import –Trade agreements can be imported by using the Microsoft Dynamics AX 2012 Application Integration Framework (AIF) or by using Microsoft Office Add-ins for Microsoft Dynamics AX 2012.

Sales prices and discounts are derived from trade agreements. This calculation can be a simple search for a valid trade agreement or a more complex calculation that finds the cheapest price and largest discount, including the concepts of generic currency and smart rounding.

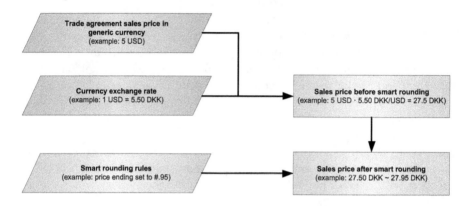

The sales prices and discounts are derived from the trade agreements when requested. This can be at the time of creating or updating a sales quotation/order, or a request can be made for exporting an electronic price list and discount list to a customer by using the Microsoft Dynamics AX 2012 Application Integration Framework (AIF).

The calculation of sales prices and discount from trade agreements is not always wanted when updating a sales quotation/order. Information is brought to the user when changes to an existing order or quotation could impact the prices and discounts that have been manually entered or transferred from another document. For example, this could be sales prices and discounts on a sales quotation/order negotiated and agreed upon during a quotation process. By displaying timely and precise information, Microsoft Dynamics AX 2012 enables the user to make conscious decisions: whether or not to keep the existing negotiated sales prices and discounts or to derive the default sales prices and discounts from the trade agreements based on the new conditions. Sales prices and discounts also can be derived from sales agreements. Sales agreements are a contract between a company and its customer. The sales prices and discounts of the sales agreement overrule any sales prices and discounts stated in any trade agreements that may exist.

Charges
In previous AX versions functionality was called "Miscellaneous charges". You can use charges to add costs to a quotation or to specific items of a quotation. Charges could be used for freight or services.
To add charges to the whole sales quotation on the Sales quotation form, in the Quotation tab on the Action Pane, click Maintain Charges in the Charges group.
To add charges to a quotation line item, select the Maintain charges option from the Sales quotation line button in the Lines Action Pane of the Sales

quotation form. This functionality works the same as it does for sales orders. Charges are copied when the quotation is confirmed to the sales order.

Working with BOMs

In the Sales quotation form, in the lines area, click Update line, select Based on BOM in the Calculate group. You can use this option to view the BOM for sales quotation line items, to update the sales price and to show the effect of quantity changes on costs.

You can use the BOM calculation option to:

- Select the options for configurable BOM items and recalculate the sales price for the item.
- Recalculate costs if raw material costs increase but are not updated in the system.
- Show the effect of quantity changes on the cost.
- Have the salesperson change the quantity and view the cost difference and margin difference based on manufacturing requirements. With this information, the salesperson can decide to offer the customer a better price on the larger quantity.

Note: This functionality works the same as it does for sales orders.

Multiple Ship To Addresses

The delivery address for a sales quotation and its line items defaults from the customer's address. However, you can set the delivery address for the whole quotation to one of the customer's alternative addresses, or have the delivery address be designated by the quotation line item. By doing this, different items from the quotation can be shipped to different customer addresses.

To designate an alternative address for the whole quotation, click the Header view in the Show group on the Action Pane and in the Address FastTab, click the Delivery address drop-down list and select a new record. If the address is not listed, click the Add icon and type a new address, or click the Select different address icon and select an address.

To designate an alternative address for a quotation line, select the Line view in the Show group on the Action Pane and in the Line details FastTab select the Address tab. The options for selecting an address are the same as the header.

Note: This functionality works the same as it does for sales orders.

Include Quotations in Master Scheduling

System can and should take into account the possibility that the sales quotations can be won, and thus they become real demand, so to make sure that the items in sales quotations are in stock if these are won, a checkmark (Include quotation) should be activated in the Master plans form in the Master Planning module (please see the Application box at the beginning of this chapter).

Price Simulation
Select a sales quotation from the All Quotations list page and then click Price simulation on the Quotation tab in the Action Pane.
Use the Run price simulation form to create a price simulation for a selected quotation header or a single quotation line, by modifying the discount percentage, margin or contribution ratio. After the simulation is run, you can compare the current quotation totals to the simulated totals and apply price simulation. The following figure shows the effect of a 15 percent discount on a sales quotation.

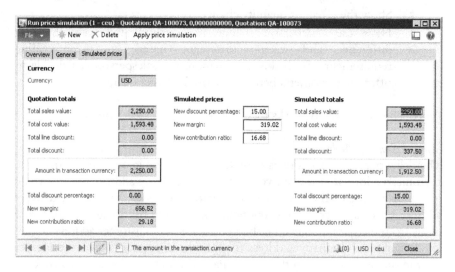

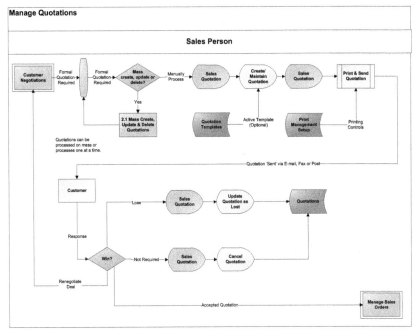

Source: Microsoft documentation

5 SALES ORDERS

An efficient sales order process is essential to every organization that is engaged in selling goods and services. Sales order efficiency helps organizations deliver strong, consistent customer service and helps reduce costs by automating and optimizing sales procedures.

Microsoft Dynamics AX 2012 enables organizations to take and process customer orders rapidly while ensuring that internal process controls and externally agreed-upon terms and conditions will be seamlessly integrated into the process. Multi-currency and multi-language support is an integral part of sales ordering in Microsoft Dynamics AX 2012 and assists organizations in selling products in a global environment.

When you enter sales orders into Microsoft Dynamics AX 2012, the system automatically checks credit limits, customer account information, and inventory levels so you can give your customers real-time information. Because sales order status and related business information is readily accessible in Microsoft Dynamics AX 2012, you can easily respond to customer inquiries. By leveraging print management, you can print, fax, or send email to dedicated destinations. You can also publish order confirmations on the web by using Microsoft Dynamics AX 2012 Enterprise Portal.

Microsoft Dynamics AX 2012 supports a variety of order entry scenarios to fulfill numerous business requirements. The focus of these scenarios ranges from tightly integrated collaborative business-to-business relations that use the Application Integration Framework (AIF), to customers on the self-service portal, sales representatives on the Enterprise Portal, and users who perform Microsoft Dynamics AX 2012 client-based order entry when a sales order is processed.

Sales Order Entry

Microsoft Dynamics AX 2012 supports sales order entry in the following ways:

- Performs comprehensive price calculations based on trade agreements.
- Automatically substitutes alternative items for unavailable items.
- Automatically enforces credit limit controls against customer credit limits.
- Automatically performs order promising at the line item level and checks inventory levels to provide customers with real-time delivery information.
- Applies customer-specific line level information such as item numbering and descriptions.
- Automatically applies negotiated terms and conditions from sales agreements at the time of order entry, in cases where long term sales agreements and schedules have been negotiated with the customer.
- Applies delivery schedules to line items, ensuring that price-related information for the sales order line can be separated from the means of delivery.
- Allows a single sales order entry for all line items, including items carried in inventory, items not carried in inventory, services, and unique, user-described items that are not on the master product list.
- Supports computer-to-computer order entry by using AIF, on Enterprise Portal, and in the Microsoft Dynamics AX 2012 client.
- Supports role-specific order entry, allowing customers to enter orders directly on the customer self-service portal.
- Automatically creates an order from confirmed sales quotations and projects.
- Enables draft sales orders, released and acknowledged sales orders, credit notes, recurring sales orders, and call-off orders from sales agreements.

After a sales order has been entered into the system, its status can be converted from "draft" to "sales order acknowledgement", which releases the order for warehouse picking and subsequent outbound operations. Dedicated list pages track the progress of a sales order through the system and ensure easy and efficient order processing.

Sales Order Processing

Microsoft Dynamics AX 2012 supports the sales order processing with a number of key features:

- Seamless integration with sales order fulfillment and billing provides the user with a comprehensive view of order fulfillment and billing - down to the line item level - when a sales order is processed.
- Dedicated list pages such as the "All sales orders", "Open sales orders", "Delayed shipments", and "Shipped but not invoiced sales orders" pages enable users to easily track the various stages in the sales order process.
- Delivery date control provides order simulation that allows users to simulate "what-if" scenarios when changing the delivery method and shipping point.
- Flexible supply options such as drop shipment, purchase to order (with and without intercompany), deliver from stock, and configure to order are available from the order line.
- Automatic or manual addition of charges such as freight or handling fees to the sales order and sales order lines.
- Print management ensures that the preferred way of exchanging order documents, such as sending a sales order acknowledgement to the customer, is always applied.
- Acceptance parameters are automatically applied for over-delivery or under-delivery.
- Automatic revenue accrual on shipment of the order.
- Event-based notifications can be configured and automatically sent to users (by using alerts) to follow up on orders and order line items.

Sales Order Global support

With its multi-currency, multi-language, multi-site capabilities, Microsoft Dynamics AX 2012 has intrinsic support for selling in a global environment. The key areas that support global sales include:

- Comprehensive support for sales tax calculation. The Microsoft Dynamics AX 2012 tax engine supports region-specific and country-specific sales taxes calculation. The tax engine also provides multiple options for defining sales tax per product, sales tax exclusions for specific industries, and reporting of individual sales taxes to separate tax authorities. Complex calculations such as "sales tax on sales tax" and "sales prices inclusive of sales tax" are also supported.

- Multi-currency support. Enables organizations to sell to a single customer using multiple currencies, and to maintain a balance in each currency.
- Multi language support. Allows users to format external, customer-facing documents and document content according to the language specified for the recipient of the document.
- Multiple address support. Ensures the separation of billing and delivery addresses on sales order lines.
- Integration with payment services for credit card processing, Includes preauthorization, authorization, and data tracking; payment services are directly integrated within Microsoft Dynamics AX 2012 processes.

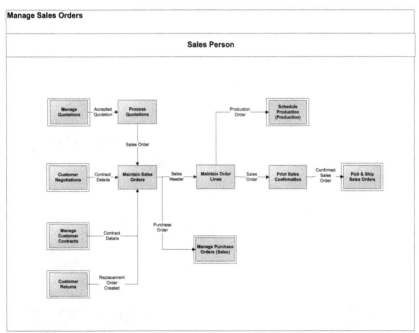

Source: Microsoft documentation

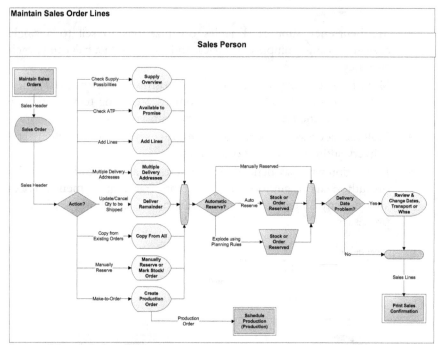

Source: Microsoft documentation

Sales Trade Agreement

The ability to execute the sales order processing according to the terms and conditions in sales agreements is essential for a business that negotiates large quantities or payments to be fulfilled, not in a single order, but in smaller amounts over time.

Microsoft Dynamics AX 2012 offers functionality to ensure that a sale conforms to these agreements when a sales order is automatically generated.

Microsoft Dynamics AX 2012 helps track sales orders that use a sales agreement, so it's easy to determine whether the fulfillment has been met before expiration of the agreement.

Microsoft Dynamics AX 2012 supports managing long-term sell-related terms, conditions, and commitments made with customers. Sales agreements can be entered directly in the system or can be generated based on an awarded request for quotation (RFQ) where an agreement has been made with the vendor.

The sales agreement includes the following capabilities:
- The agreement can be for one customer.
- The agreement can consists of one or more commitments. The commitments can be of different types within the same agreement.

Four types of commitments express the obligation to sell:

- For a specific quantity of a product. The sales of the product happen over a period of time and the quantity on the order lines must add up to the quantity specified in the agreement[9]. A unit price and, for example, a discount are applied to the order.
- For a specific monetary amount of a product. The sales of the product happen over a period of time and the line amount on the order lines must add up to the amount specified in the agreement. A line discount can be applied to the order; for example, an agreement for an up-front 5 percent line discount on the product Home Theater System.
- For a specific monetary amount within a specific sales category. The sales within the category happen over a period of time and the line amount on the order lines must add up to the amount specified in the agreement. A line discount can be applied to the order; for example, an agreement for an up-front line discount of 10 percent for sales within the category "office furniture."
- For a specific amount of any sale, regardless of products or categories. The sales happen over a period of time and the line amount on the order lines must add up to the amount specified in the agreement. A line discount can be applied to the order; for example, an agreement for an up-front line discount of 3 percent on any sale.

Each commitment has a time period in which it should be fulfilled and the agreement terms on the commitment cannot be used beyond the validity period determined by the requested ship date on the sales order.

- The agreement has an Agreement classification.
- Each agreement has terms for payment, delivery address, mode of delivery, and more, which are agreed upon with the customer. These terms are copied to the sales order when used.
- Each agreement holds data relevant to the internal processing of sales orders; for example, a sales commission group, which is copied to the sales order.
- The agreement can allow the committed amount or quantity to be exceeded, so the agreement can be used even if the total sold quantity or monetary amount exceeds the committed level.

---

[9] This type of agreement was called Blanket order in the Microsoft Dynamics AX 2009 version.

- An agreement can be used in an intercompany trading relationship and is synchronized in both companies. If the agreement is used in one company, it is automatically used by the intercompany order in the other company.
- An agreement can be related to a specific project and used when selling within the scope of that project.

Using a trade agreement in order process

An agreement can be applied to the sales and purchase order process in the following ways, depending on the business requirements: automatically, semi-automatically, or manually.

Automatically. The following scenarios illustrate when an agreement is automatically applied:

- In firming[10] a planned order.
- In a purchase order generated from a production order.
- In a purchase order generated from a sales order, including the direct delivery scenario[11].
- In purchases generated from a purchase requisition.

Semi-automatically. The user entering the order from the customer or vendor cart is notified if the customer or vendor has agreements that are available to use.

Manually. When a user creates the sales or purchase order directly from the list page or detail page of orders, the agreement must be selected during the creation process. The user is presented with a list of possible agreements that can be used for the specific customer or vendor. Alternatively, the sales order can be created directly from the agreement.

When a new line is added to an order that is associated with an agreement, the system automatically searches the commitments in the agreement and applies the terms in the agreement if there is a match. There is full visibility from the order and the order line to the related agreement and the commitment that is being fulfilled.

---

[10] Firming a planned order means transforming a planned order purchase/production order into purchase/production orders

[11] AX allows direct creation of purchase orders from the sales order (purchase-to-order)

Using the Sales or Purchase Agreement

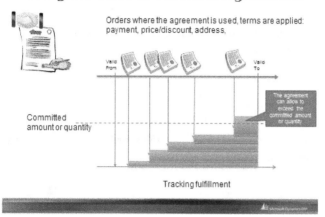

Orders where the agreement is used, terms are applied: payment, price/discount, address,

Source: Microsoft documentation

Follow-up on Sales Agreement

Microsoft Dynamics AX 2012 supports tracking the fulfillment rate by visualizing the states of the order lines in relation to the actual quantity or amount remaining, released, received or delivered, and invoiced.

The system provides drilldown capabilities from the commitment to the orders and invoices that fulfill the commitment.

The fulfillment report allows for following up on multiple commitments on agreements where it's possible to filter out commitments that are close to expiration.

Sales Order Form

The Sales order form is used to enter and view the details about one specific sales order. There are several methods to open the Sales order form:

- Open Sales and marketing > Common > Sales orders > All sales orders. Next, click Sales order in the New group of the Action Pane.
- Open Sales and marketing > Common > Customers > All customers. Next, click Sales order in the New group on the Sell tab of the Action Pane.
- Open Sales and marketing > Common > Sales orders > All sales orders. Next, select the desired sales order and then click Edit in the Maintain group of the Action Pane.
- Open Sales and marketing > Common > Sales orders > All sales orders. Next, double-click the desired sales order.

The Sales order form has the following views available: header view, line view, and edit in grid view.

Sales Order Statuses
A sales order can have several statuses that indicate how far the selected order is within the sales order process.
- Open order
- Received
- Invoiced
- Canceled

In addition to the status on the header of the sales order, each line of the order can also have a status, as follows:
- Open order
- Received
- Invoiced
- Canceled

Sales Order Document Statuses
In addition to the sales order status, each sales order has a document status that indicates which documents are generated for a selected sales order.
- None - no documents are generated for the order.
- Confirmation - a confirmation is generated for the order.
- Picking list - at least one picking list is generated for the order.
- Packing slip- at least one packing slip is generated for the order.
- Invoice - at least one invoice is generated for the order.

Because the status and document status are calculated separately, different combinations of statuses and document status can help additionally identify an order's status. For example, if an order's status is Open order and the document status is Invoice, you can conclude that the order is partly received and invoiced.

One-Time Customer
Use the One-time customer function when you are working with a customer who does not exist in the Customer form. Before you use this function, make sure that a number sequence is set up for one-time customers in Account receivable > Setup > Account receivable parameters > Number sequences.

Sales Order Types
When you create a sales order in Microsoft Dynamics AX 2012, select from one of several sales order types:
- Journal

- Subscription
- Sales Order

You cannot select the following sales order types manually, because they are created through the Return management feature or the Project management and accounting module:

- Returned Order
- Item Requirements

Sales Order

The sales order type of Sales order is used when the customer places or confirms that he or she wants the items/services. You can set the default type to be Sales order inside the Accounts Receivable Parameters form, depending on the client's business process.

Journal

Sales orders of the Journal type are used as draft sales orders, usually entered by junior, new or temporary workers (operators) as an intermediate step before the order is firm. Journals help when you bring data into the system that might not meet quality or other standards. The sales order of Journal type has no effect on stock quantities and does not generate item transactions, thus it does not create demand for master planning.

Subscription

The sales order type of Subscription is used for repeated/recurring sales of the same item or service to the same customer. When a packing slip is updated, Microsoft Dynamics AX 2012 generates a packing slip. When the invoice is updated, a new packing slip or invoice entry can be updated for the same sales line. The order's status is never Invoiced, only Open or Delivered.

Returned order

The sales order type of Returned order is used when you receive goods back from a customer. The Returned order type in Microsoft Dynamics AX 2012 cannot be selected manually. A return material number (aka RMA number) is assigned automatically and can be viewed on the Other tab. It is created through the Return orders form in Sales and marketing > Common > Return orders > All return orders.

Item Requirements

The sales order type of Item requirements is connected to the Microsoft Dynamics AX 2012 Project management and accounting module. When you create the item requirements in the Project management and accounting module, the system automatically creates a sales order of the type Item requirements, with a reference to the project number.

Creating Sales Order
There are several ways to create a sales order. Creation of a sales order can be made from the sales order lists by selecting the customer and entering the sales details or from the customer form. Creating a sales order from the Customer form will skip the Sales order create form and all defaults from the customer will be transferred automatically.

Enter Sales Order Header details
Detailed information can be entered or viewed for a sales order by using the Header view or Lines view[12] on the Sales order form. To enter details about a sales order, select the desired sales order and then click Edit in the Maintain group of the Action Pane, click Header view in the Show group of the Sales order form (or click F12) and then click in each tab to enter the required information.

Adding lines to a sales order
There are several ways that you can add lines to a sales order.
- *Manually* add one line at a time by using the Add line button on the Sales order lines tab, or enter Ctrl +N when focused on a line, and then select one of the following:
  - o *Item number*: Use the Item number drop-down list to select a product that is defined in the system. These products can be services or items, and might be stocked or not stocked based on the setup that is defined on the product.
  - o *Sales category*: Select the category from the sales category hierarchy. For lines with internally-defined product numbers, the category derives from the setup in the product catalog. For lines without product numbers, the category is selected on the order line.
- *Add multiple lines* by using the Add lines button on the Sales order lines tab. On the Create lines form, use the Filter > Advanced filter sort button to search for the desired products. Next, enter the desired quantity next to each item number in the Sales quantity field. Use the Create button to accept the amounts and close the form, or use the Apply button to add the selected item numbers to the sales order and continue to search.

---

[12] This is another interface change in Microsoft Dynamics AX 2012. User can view either header details or lines details.

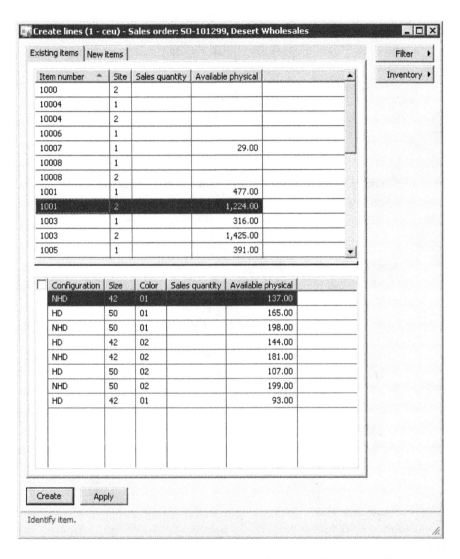

- *Copy lines* from another sales order by using the From all or From journal button in the Copy group of the Action Pane on the Sales order form.
- There are several differences on a sales order lines when the product is a stocked product, a not stocked product, or a sales category base line.
- Sales category base line: site is mandatory and the warehouse is optional. Only site and warehouse can be entered on the order line.

- Not stocked products: site is mandatory, other storage and tracking dimensions are active according to the dimension group setup. However, they are optional.
- Stocked products: site is mandatory and other storage and tracking dimensions are active and can be mandatory, depending on the dimension group setup.

Note: If a line item is sales category based, then foreign trade information must be manually entered for the order line.

Copy from All

When you create a sales order, the Copy from all feature lets you view all sales orders, confirmations, packing slips, and invoice lines to select a document or lines that are most like the one(s) being created. This data can be copied and used as a starting point for a new sales order.

This helps when you create a new sales order that resembles one that was created for a different customer, or even for the same customer for a different item or quantity. Within this option, users can configure the copying of these variables in the Quantity and Setup field groups:

- Quantity factor
- Invert sign
- Copy charges
- Recalculate price
- Copy precisely
- Delete order lines
- Copy order header

You can open the Copy from all form by clicking Copy from all in the Copy group of the Action Pane or in the Sales order lines tab of the Line view, and then clicking Sales order line and selecting an option for copying information.

Ship to Multiple Addresses

The Multiple ship to functionality lets users specify delivery addresses for each order line instead of only according to the order header.

Use the Multiple ship to functionality in sales orders to perform the following actions:

- Specify multiple customer delivery addresses on sales order lines.
- Copy addresses that are manually entered on the sales order into the Addresses table for reuse later.
- Select if sales order documents are printed for each delivery address or for each order.

Delivery Schedules

In Microsoft Dynamics AX 2012, delivery schedules are used on the sales order and sales quotation. This lets the user split an order line into multiple deliveries.

The delivery schedule consists of an order line with multiple deliveries that are manifested as delivery schedule lines. Each delivery schedule line is displayed in the sales order below the order line with multiple deliveries. An icon distinguishes between the order line with multiple deliveries and the delivery schedule lines.

The order line with multiple deliveries serves as a template for the delivery schedule lines. This means that when the delivery schedule lines are created, the values are copied from the order line with multiple deliveries to the delivery schedule lines.

For example, prices and conditions from trade agreements will be applied to the order line with multiple deliveries and copied to the delivery schedule lines.

The quantity of the order line with multiple deliveries and the sum of the quantity of the delivery schedule lines will always be synchronized. After a delivery schedule line is created, most of the attributes of the delivery line can be edited as on a typical order line.

Only delivery schedule lines will be displayed on the sales order confirmation or picking lists, not the order line with multiple deliveries.

Note: You can delete a delivery schedule from the Delivery schedule form. If you delete the order line, the delivery schedule will also be deleted.

Enhanced Delivery Date Control

The Enhanced delivery date control function is primarily about giving realistic and complete delivery promises to a customer during sales order entry and shortening the sales order entry time.

Enhanced delivery date control supports the user in his or her daily work and makes it simpler to give realistic delivery dates. The order processor enters sales orders and Microsoft Dynamics AX 2012 checks if the requested delivery date for the customer can be met from a shipping perspective. If a requested delivery date cannot be met, the order processor is provided with user-friendly simulation that lists the options to help find a resolution to the requested delivery date problem.

Use the delivery date control function together with transfer orders, where the delivery date control is used to calculate earliest possible ship and receipt dates for the transfer order/transfer order lines.

Enhanced delivery date control examines:

- Various levels at which the delivery date control can be enabled;

- The range of factors to include in the delivery data calculation to give you the most accurate delivery date;
- Using the Available dates functionality to simulate different delivery scenarios and accept or reject calculated delivery dates.

Enable the Delivery Date Control Feature

To enable default delivery date control on the sales order header, you must enable the feature. Do this by selecting Sales lead time in the Delivery date control parameter in Accounts receivable > Setup > Accounts receivable parameters > Shipments tab.

Enabling the Delivery date control feature helps you make sure that delivery date control is set by default every time that you create a sales order header.

You can set up delivery date control on each item, in the Default order setting form, and this defaults to the sales order lines, even if the Delivery date control parameter setting is None. The Delivery date control setting on the item overrides the parameter setting

You can also enable the Delivery date control function at various points in the sales order creation process:

- Create sales order
- Sales order header
- Sales order lines
- Create release order

Note: If you select the ATP, CTP or ATP + Issue margin in the Delivery date control parameter, it will work with the Available-to-promise (ATP) time fence and ATP incl. planned orders parameters for the ATP feature.

Available-to-Promise

The available-to-promise (ATP) parameter is available in the Delivery date control field in the Accounts receivable parameters and on the Default order settings form on the item setup.

Available-to-promise (ATP) logic applies to stocked items, and automatically results in the assignment of a delivery date to a sales order line item. ATP logic assumes that item replenishment is driven by demand procurement and production. Therefore, delivery promises can be based on scheduled receipts within the horizon that is defined by the ATP time fence. The optional consideration of planned orders as scheduled receipts would be applicable when most planned orders are used to create actual supply orders.

The ATP time fence for an item typically represents its cumulative lead time, although it sometimes represents the lead time to produce a manufactured item from stocked components. The promised delivery date will be automatically placed at the end of the time horizon that is defined by the ATP time fence when there are insufficient scheduled receipts.

The ATP logic can also consider past-due demand and supply. These dates should be updated to the current date or a future date to correctly coordinate supply chain activities, either by manually changing the date or by automatic changes based on the calculated futures date. When the dates are not updated, the optional ATP policies should be used to consider the past-due dates. For example, past due demand and supplies might be considered for the past three days to cover those situations in which you have not yet updated the dates.

Capable-to-Promise

Capable-to-promise (CTP) logic generally applies to make-to-order items, and automatically results in the assignment of a delivery date to a sales order line item. CTP logic considers components' on-hand inventories and their lead times to suggest a promised delivery date. For example, when no component inventory exists, the promised delivery date reflects the item's cumulative manufacturing lead time.

The CTP logic is conceptually similar to the explosion logic for a sales line. The Explosion logic must be manually invoked for a line item, and involves several steps to correctly calculate and update the promised delivery date on a sales line.

Earliest Possible Delivery Date Factors

Several factors can help determine the earliest possible delivery date to the customer when you use the delivery date control functionality. Microsoft Dynamics AX 2012 uses certain factors to base its calculation of the earliest possible delivery date for a sales order.

When calculating the earliest possible delivery date, the system considers the following factors: delivery date control method (None, Sales lead time, ATP, ATP + Issue margin or CTP), coverage calendar, order deadlines, transport time, transport calendars, customer receipt calendars.

Sales Lead Time

Sales lead time is the number of days that you can use on all the activities from receiving the sales order to shipping it. These activities can include sales administration tasks, conducting checks on items before shipping them, warehouse administration tasks, etc.

The sales lead time is a default value for all items that you sell from your company. However, notice that the sales lead time on individual items overrides the sales lead time in the Accounts receivable parameters[13].

Considering the sales lead time, if you try to specify a requested shipping date that falls before the first possible date, the system generates a warning and asks you to find another available date for delivery.

The system-proposed ship and receipt dates can be overridden if you click Disable dlv. date control button. In this case, the system accepts the dates that were originally proposed, although you cannot force the system to accept a closed date in the calendar or a date in the past.

Coverage Calendar

The coverage calendar for the warehouse is set up for each warehouse. In the coverage calendar, you can set up open and closed days for the warehouse. If the requested shipping date falls on a closed day, then the next open day is used for the requested shipping date. If you do not set up a coverage calendar, the open and closed days for the company are defined in the Company information form on the Shipping calendar.

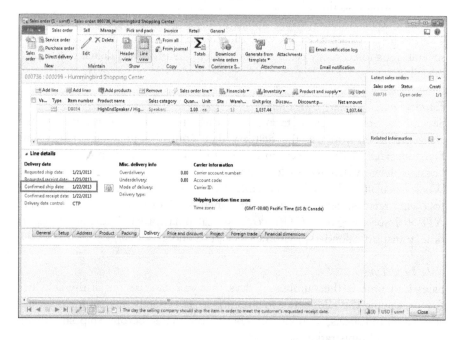

---

[13] Define the sales order lead time in Accounts receivable > Setup > Accounts receivable parameters > Shipments tab.

Transport Time

Set up transport time between a warehouse in your company and a customer address in the Transport form. This is opened by clicking Inventory and warehouse management > Setup > Distribution > Transport.

Note: Make sure that fallback warehouses are associated with the sites. The fallback warehouse is used to calculate the transport time if a site but no warehouse is specified on the sales order line.

Fallback Warehouse

The Transport form is controlled based on warehouse and not site. This means that if only the site is specified on the sales order line, the Transport form does not receive the necessary input to calculate and find the correct transport time.

The Fallback warehouse for site form is where you can specify a fallback warehouse for a site. This means that if only the site is specified on a sales order line, the necessary information for the Transport form is pulled from the fallback warehouse for that specific site instead. Therefore, the Transport form still calculates the transport time based on the individual warehouse settings.

Note: The fallback warehouse settings also apply if transport has only been set up for Warehouse A on a site and Warehouse B is selected on the sales order line.

Transport Calendar

A transport calendar can be attached to a Mode of delivery by opening the transport calendar from the Modes of delivery form in Accounts receivable > Setup > Distribution.

The transport calendar lets you operate either with Mode of delivery, either Warehouse specific.

The transport calendar is a working time calendar and allows for three statuses of the working times, which are:
- Open - the mode of delivery is open for pickup and delivery.
- Closed - the mode of delivery is closed for pickup and delivery.
- Closed for pickup - this means that the carrier can operate on an open day but does not make pickups from warehouses on that day. This is an important feature because many carriers operate seven days a week but might only pick up items to be delivered on certain days of the week.

Supply Overview

The purpose of the Supply overview form in Microsoft Dynamics AX 2012 is to provide an overview of the available supply beyond the default supply option and to enable the user to view and compare the alternatives for supplying items that the customer requires at the time that he or she specified. These can be other sites (besides the site making the delivery), vendors that are rarely used, alternative ways of producing the item.

To satisfy a customer's demand for an item, the item can frequently be sourced in many ways, by creating a production order at the site from which the order will be shipped to the customer, by using available items in inventory or on existing production orders or purchased orders, by creating a new purchase order or by transferring from other warehouses. For some items, all those options are available; for others items, only a subset can be used.

Available Ship and Receipt Dates

The Available ship and receipt dates dialog box appears if a sales order cannot be delivered on the requested date, considering all the calendars and times that you have previously set up.

Available Ship and Receive Date Dialog Box

The Available ship and receipt dates form provides an immediate and clear warning that indicates if you can deliver a sales order in time to meet the customer's requirements.

In the Available ship and receipt dates form, you can perform the following:

- View the dates on which you can/cannot ship a sales order in the upper part of the form and the reason why the date is unavailable. For example, the shipping date falls on a closed date in the transport calendar.
- Resolve the problem. For example, change the mode of delivery for the order.

The most important prerequisite for using the Available dates functionality is that the Delivery date control parameter is selected.

Specify and Update Request Dates with the Available Dates Function

When you create a sales order, Microsoft Dynamics AX 2012 calculates the earliest possible ship date and receipt date. The earliest ship and receipt dates depend on the setup that is created for all the factors previously referred to in the "Enhanced Delivery Date Control".

If you try to select a requested ship date or requested receipt date that falls before the calculated requested ship date or requested receipt date, the Available ship and receipt dates dialog box appears.

The Available ship and receipt dates form has two panes:

- Top pane: indicates what the problem is with the requested ship/receipt date for the selected sales order.
- Bottom pane: the non-available dates are indicated with a caution icon. These are likely closed days in the calendar. The rest of the dates are available.

Order Entry Deadlines

The delivery date control feature lets you specify order entry deadlines for each site and considers that sites might be located in different time zones. This deadline in Microsoft Dynamics AX 2012 is defined as the order entry deadline. The order entry deadline is defined for each site according to the time zone that the site is located in and not the time zone where sales orders are created. In addition, you can enable certain important customers to have later order entry deadlines than other customers.

In many companies, a sales order must be received before a certain time of day for the sales order to be treated as if it is received that day. If the order is received after this deadline, the company treats the sales order as if it is received the next business day.

Direct Delivery

Microsoft Dynamics AX 2012 supports direct delivery to customers. With direct delivery, sales orders are delivered directly from the vendor to the customer without physically entering your company's inventory.

The direct delivery functionality in Microsoft Dynamics AX 2012 has the following advantages over the traditional non-direct delivery distribution supply chain:

- Reduced time from when you create sales orders to the delivery to the customer.
- No inventory carrying or labor costs because the items never physically enter inventory.
- Reduced transportation costs because the items go directly from the vendor to the customer.
- Reduced administration time and less chance of order entry error because purchase orders are directly created from the sales order and there is a single point to update delivery/receipt of orders.

When you create a sales order for direct delivery, all document updates from the sales order are unavailable, except the Confirmation and Invoice. The Invoice is available only when the order has reached a status of delivered. All posting updates concerned with delivery of items to the customer, except

Confirmation, are performed from the purchase order. This makes sure that product receipt updates for the purchase order and its attached sales order are synchronized.

Synchronization between orders reduces the probability of order processors updating the purchase order's packing slip but not the sales order packing slip, reduces delays between updating the purchase order and sales order, reduces the probability of a purchase order being updated against the wrong sales order or the wrong quantities being updated between the purchase order and sales order.

By using this synchronized updating process, you make sure that packing slip updates of purchase orders are reflected in the update of the attached sales order.

Process Flow - Direct Delivery

The Process Flow in a Direct Delivery Sales Order figure shows the process flow in a direct delivery sales order from the customer's initial call through the final invoicing of the sales order.

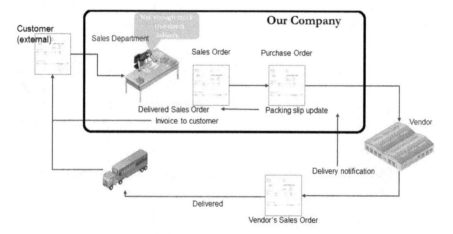

Updating Sales Orders

When you update a Sales order/Sales order lines, corresponding updates appear on the attached Purchase order/Purchase order lines. Similarly, when you update a Purchase order/Purchase order lines, corresponding updates appear on the attached Sales order/Sales order lines.

The system treat this construct as a whole, thus the updates on Sales Orders determines a reaction on a Purchase Order:

- When updating the address on sales order line, the address is updated on corresponding purchase order line.

- When updating the Requested shipping date on sales order line of direct delivery type, the Delivery date is updated on corresponding purchase order line.
- When updating the quantity on sales order line, the Quantity is updated on corresponding purchase order line.
- When deleting sales order line, the system allows to choose if the corresponding purchase order line is to be deleted.
- When creating a new sales order line of the direct delivery type a new purchase order of direct delivery type is created in the Purchase orders form.

Similarly, when updating Purchase Order the system determines reactions on a Sales Order:

- When updating part delivery of a purchase order line, the delivered quantity is updated in the sales order line
- When updating Confirmed delivery date on the purchase order line, the Confirmed ship date on the sales order line is updated

View Related Orders

There are several ways to identify and trace purchase orders and purchase order lines that are related to a sales order. On the General tab of the Sales order form, there are two buttons in the Related information group: References and Purchase orders. The Purchase order button opens the Purchase order form, displaying the purchase order that is related to the sales order. This button is available only when a sales order is related to a purchase order.

Processing a Sales Order

You can apply various techniques for processing a sales order when you work with sales orders in Microsoft Dynamics AX 2012.

The document generation options are as follows:

- Confirmation
- Picking list
- Picking list registration
- Packing slip

In Microsoft Dynamics AX 2012, you also have the option to use the Pro-forma documents from the Sales order. This means that the Posting check box will be inactivated by default, and pro-forma papers can be printed.

The ability to use all order postings depends on the specific needs of a company.

Generate a Sales Order Confirmation

After you create a sales order, generate (post) the sales order confirmation to confirm the details of the order and send a confirmation of the sales order to the customer.

This step does not change the order's status. The Document status is updated to Confirmed and the system creates a Confirmation journal.

Sales orders can be confirmed individually or in bulk. You also have the option to print a pro forma sales order. This lets you view the details before confirming and sending it to the customer.

Confirm Sales Order Form - Print Options

In the Print options field group, select the printing options for confirmation. Specify if you want to print the confirmation and use the print management system. The print management system works the same for the sales order as it does for purchase orders.

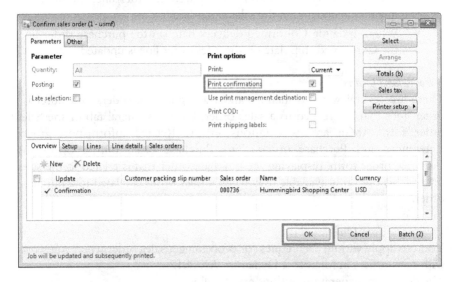

Confirm Sales Order Form - Parameters

The Parameters field group contains three check boxes that control what is to be posted and when.

- Quantity - This parameter lets you specify the quantity that you want the order to update. The only option available for the Confirm sales order form is All, meaning that you can only confirm the whole order quantities.
- Posting - Select to post the confirmation. Clear this field to create a pro forma confirmation. Creating a pro forma confirmation is useful

if you want to view and review the confirmation before you send it to the customer.

- Late selection - Clear the parameter unless you intend to process the order at a later date through a batch.

Confirm Sales Order Form - Other Tab
The Other tab has two field groups:
- Setup
- Summary update

In the Setup field group, start a credit check on the customer and set a deadline date to delimit the transaction.

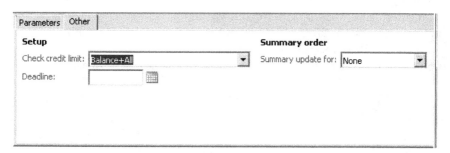

Check Credit Limit Options
There are multiple options available when you want to run the check credit limit check when you post a sales order, depending on the policy selected in Accounts receivable > Setup > Accounts receivable parameters> Check credit limit for a sales order:

- None - No credit limit check is performed unless a setting is selected in Accounts receivable > Setup > Accounts receivable parameters> Check credit limit for a sales order. If this is the case, a credit limit check is performed when you create the order.
- Balance - A credit limit check is performed against the balance for a customer.
- Balance+Packing slip - A credit limit check is performed against the balance for a customer and the value for any packing slip updated order.
- Balance+All - A credit limit is performed against the balance for a customer, the value of any packing slip updated orders, and any open orders.

Depending on the parameter setup in Accounts receivable parameters, when running a credit limit check on the order and the credit limit is exceeded, a warning or an error is generated. With a warning you can still continue with the update, while an error prevents update.

Confirm Sales Order Form - Summary Update
Summary update in sales orders works similarly to summary update for purchase orders. Summary updating for sales orders for the various summary update settings is described below:
- None - No summary updates will be made. This means one order and one confirmation.
- Invoice account - Summary update will be made for the selected sales orders by their invoice account.

Example
You select four sales orders for update and of these four, two have one invoice account specified for them and the other two have another invoice account specified for them. If you perform an Invoice account summary update for the orders, two invoices are created, one for each invoice account.

- Automatic summary - Summarize all selected orders according to the criteria that is set in the Summary update parameters form, but only if summary updating is specified in the Summary update form. If not, the order will be posted separately.

Confirm Sales Order Form - Lower Panel
The lower panel of the Posting confirmation form contains five tabs:
- Overview
- Setup
- Lines
- Line details
- Sales orders

Confirm Sales Order Form - Overview Tab. On the lower panel of the Confirm sales order form, you can review the details on the Overview tab to make sure that you are processing the correct sales order. The yellow caution triangle or tick, indicates if an order can be updated. Notice that this is a high level validation and only indicates if the order will post or not.
Confirm Sales Order Form - Setup Tab. On the Setup tab of the Confirm sales order form, you can enter the Date of confirmation if it differs from today's date.
Confirm Sales Order Form - Lines and Line Details Tab. When you select the Lines tab, you can review that the items and quantities are correct. Click the

Inventory button to access functions such as picking and reservation from the update for the line.

You can view additional details on each line by selecting the Line details tab. When you are satisfied that all sales orders, item criteria, and quantities are correct, click the OK button to generate the order confirmation.

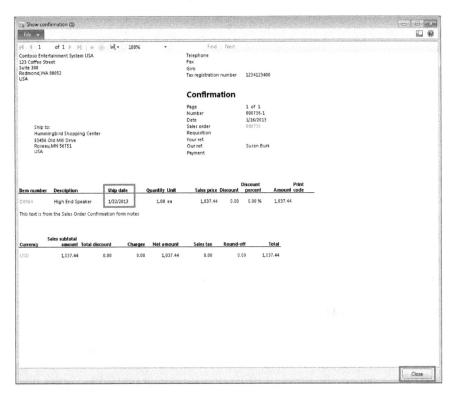

Generate a Sales Order Picking List

The second step in updating sales orders is to generate the sales order picking list. When and if you run a picking list update, it is either voluntary or mandatory, depending on the item model attached to the item that you are selling. If the Picking requirement parameter is selected in Inventory and warehouse management > Setup > Inventory > Item model group, the sales order line must have the status of Picked before you can continue to packing slip update the line.

Picking List Generation and Parameters

The ability to use the Picking requirement function depends on if you use the Warehouse management (WMS) functionality. When WMS is not used, the picking process depends on the setting in the Picking route status field in Accounts receivable > Setup > Accounts receivable parameters.

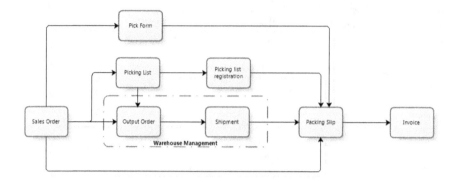

Posting Picking List Form - *Quantity Field*

In the Quantity field, specify the quantity with which you want the order updated. How update quantities works resembles the Quantity settings in the purchase order updates, except that sales order quantities deal with the issue of items instead of their receipt.

Posting Picking List Form - *Parameters Tab*

The posting and printing options for posting and printing a picking list are almost the same as the options for posting and printing a confirmation (see above sections). Additionally, on the Parameters tab, you can select or clear the Reduce quantity check box.

If Reduce quantity is Selected, you can select the Reduce quantity check box to reduce the quantity to be picked to the available on-hand quantity of the item. This resolves the problem of picking lists being printed for order lines where quantities of the item are not in stock. Instead, a picking list is only generated for available quantities of the item.

If Reduce quantity is Clear, the pick list will be created for the whole requested quantity, not only the available on-hand inventory.

Posting Picking List Form - *Other Tab*

In addition to the settings that are available on the Confirmation update, on the Other tab of the Posting picking list, you will find a Reservation parameter. If the status of Reservation parameter is Selected, when you run a Picking list update, items are automatically reserved. If it's Clear, when you run the Picking list update, items will not be reserved. This status has implications for which quantities of items can be picked for other sales order lines.

Process a Picking List Registration

When the Picking route status field is set to Activated in Accounts receivable > Setup > Account receivable Parameters on the Updates tab, you can perform a Picking list registration after you post the Picking list to register the physical pick of the sales order and have a tighter control of where the sales order is in the order process.

Generate a Sales Order Packing Slip

When the item is ready to ship to the customer, you will post a packing slip. When you have posted the packing slip, the system recognizes that the sales order demand is satisfied and reduces the physical on-hand inventory, if you have not performed the Picking list registration.

If Picking list registration is performed, it is at that time that the system will reduce the physical on-hand inventory.

To generate a sales order packing slip, follow these steps open Sales and marketing > Common > Sales orders > All sales order, select the sales order to generate the packing slip, go to the Pick and pack tab of the Action Pane, click Packing slip in the Generate group. The Packing slip posting form opens. In the Posting packing slip form, in the Quantity field, select the All option, select the Print packing slip check box to print the packing slip and click OK on the Posting dialog box.

If the quantities on the packing slip update equal the ordered quantities, the value in the sales order Status field changes to Delivered. If there is a back order on one or more items, the sales order status remains as Open order.

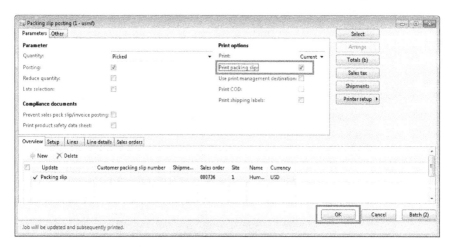

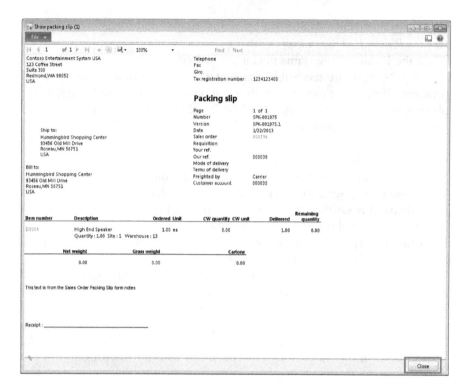

Packing Slip Posting Form

The Parameters Tab contains settings for the packing slip update which are primarily the same as the options for the Confirmation update with some exceptions.

When you select the Picked option from the list, any quantities on the sales order lines that are picked become the proposed quantity for packing slip updating.

You can select the Reduce quantity parameter to reduce the quantity to be packing slip updated to the quantity available on hand. This works the same as the Reduce quantity parameter in the picking list update, except that the parameter applies to quantities for packing slip update.

The Other Tab of the Packing Slip Posting Form shows options such as:

- Credit correction, where you can indicate whether a particular update is a correction to a transaction. Select the Credit correction check box to post the ledger transactions that are equal to the debit note ledger transactions, except for the sign. If the transactions are not equal, the debit note postings are mirrored when you post the credit note. This is used for sales orders with the Returned order type or for credit notes. Credit correction is used to track and account for a return order, if there are incorrect or damaged goods being received. Select this check box to display, for example, a credit note as a debit in your voucher transactions.

- Credit remaining quantity. Where you can select if your customer wants returned quantities to be updated to open order line quantities (back orders). If your customer does not want a new delivery of the returned items, do not select this option.

For example, you create a sales order with a customer for ten pieces of an item and invoice-update the order. Two days later, the customer calls to complain that two of the ten items are defective. You perform the following tasks:
1. Credit the customer's account by entering "-2" in the Deliver now field.
2. Click Packing slip, and in the Quantity field, select Deliver now.
3. On the Other tab, select the Credit remaining quantity check box.
When you packing slip update the negative quantity, the remaining quantity remains open for delivery at a later date. You can see this in the order header's Status field because the order status is updated to Open order.
If the Credit remaining quantity field was clear, the order status remains at Delivered and there is no back order quantity to deliver.
This functionality works in similar way for invoice updating, except that when the parameter is cleared, the status remains Invoiced and not Delivered.

Posting Packing Slip Form - Lower Panel
The settings in the lower panel of the Posting packing slip form resemble other sales order updates. However, on the Setup tab, you can enter the Packing slip date if this differs from today's date.

View Changes between Packing Slip Versions
All changes on each packing slip version are traced by the system. You can view all changes to a given packing slip on the Compare packing slip versions form.
To access this form, follow these steps:
1. Open Packing slip journal from the Sales order form, or open Sales and marketing > Inquiries > Journals > Packing slip.
2. Click History to open the Packing slip history form to show the multiple versions.
3. Click Compare versions. From the Compare packing slip versions form, you can view and compare the differences of each packing slip version.

Shipping Carrier Interface
Companies may choose to outsource transportation to specialized companies in order to reduce operating costs. In AX they can use many shipping carriers to deliver their products to customers.
The Shipment carrier interface provides integration with the shipping carrier's software to help eliminate manual entry and improve tracking visibility.

Integration with Shipping Carriers
Integration automatically moves information that is received from the shipping carriers, such as freight charges and tracking numbers, into Microsoft Dynamics AX 2012 sales orders and invoices.
A user can perform the following tasks:

- Calculate freight charges and add them to invoices as miscellaneous charges
- Facilitate a will-call[14] request by using the Sales pickup form
- Request and manage tracking numbers by generating them in the shipping carrier software and then copying them into Microsoft Dynamics AX 2012.
- Print labels with the carrier software by using address information from Microsoft Dynamics AX 2012.

---

[14] A will-call is a situation where customers buy an item beforehand and then pick it up themselves. The Sales pickup form is used to handle this type of request.

Sales flow

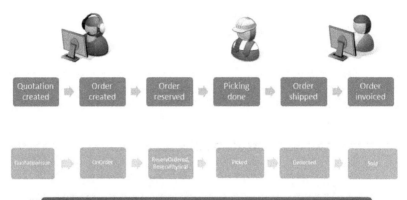

Source: Microsoft documentation

6 ITEM RESERVATIONS

Item Reservations are used by some companies to provide more accurate information on the available on-hand inventory to the salespersons or order takers. The three reservations types that are available in Microsoft Dynamics AX 2012 are manual, automatic and explosion reservations. The functionality also allows viewing and inquiring on reservations by using the lock reservations functionality, canceling and making batch reservations and also identifying the relationship between reservations and sales order picking.

The classic scenario is that a company processes hundreds of sales orders every day and the system must provide the way to ensure that a sale is accomplished when promised to customer. The sales order processors confirm that sufficient inventory is on-hand to satisfy each order as they record the orders. To make sure that the inventory sold is available when the order is picked, they use the Microsoft Dynamics AX 2012 reservations functionality. By doing this, the item(s) is (are) reserved from the time of sale onward, and the sales order processors can confirm the order and delivery date at the time of sale.

Why Perform Reservations and What Can be Reserved?
Inventory quantities can be reserved for a specific sales order. When inventory is reserved, it cannot be withdrawn from the warehouse for other orders unless the inventory reservation, or part of it, is canceled. When you perform a reservation the quantity is reserved against on-hand inventory. Depending on the Inventory management parameters settings, quantities can also be reserved against ordered, but not yet received quantities of items.

There are several reasons to reserve inventory, including the following:

- Reservations provide a historical approach for making delivery promises against on-hand inventory.

- First ordered, first delivered, means customers receive available items in the order their sales order lines are created.
- A shortage of items when there is a long, or unknown, delivery time from the vendor. Make sure certain customers or orders receive delivery of the first available items.
- Certain customers and types of orders can have first priority for delivery.
- When you work with items that have serial or batch numbers, specific serial/batch numbers can be reserved for specific orders.
- Special ordered items can be reserved for certain orders.
- When you use production orders, specific items can be reserved that are produced for specific orders, or adjusted to meet specific orders.
- When you use the Create purchase order and Create direct delivery functions from a sales order, reservations are automatically made between the sales order and the attached purchase order. The item's type determines what can be reserved from an order:
- Reserve items and Bills of Material (BOM) items. Notice that only the BOM item is reserved at reservation and not the component items.
- Items of the type Service and not stocked products cannot be reserved because there is no on-hand inventory.

Reservation, Dimensions and Transactions

When you work with reservations, inventory dimension values are important. For all item issues, inventory dimension values must be specified according to the item's dimension group before physical picking occurs. The dimension values are specified directly on the line by using the Pick dialog box, through Pick list registration, or as a reservation.

When you reserve inventory, consider these three inventory dimension types:

- Storage dimension, especially those with the Primary stocking parameter selected
- Tracking dimension
- Product dimension

Reservations apply to on-hand inventory, not to a transaction. This means reservations are created on lines in the On-hand form and not on lines in the Transactions form. Because there are on-hand inventories for each dimension value, a reservation can be created on the on-hand inventory that is specified by the issue transaction dimensions. However, if the Reserve ordered item parameter is selected, reservations can also be created on ordered but not yet received items.

Reservation Parameters
You can determine the way and what types of reservations are made by specifying the parameters to set up for reservations.

Reserve Ordered Items. If the Reserve ordered items check box is selected, items that are ordered but not yet received can be reserved. To verify the status of this parameter, open Inventory and warehouse management > Setup > Inventory and warehouse management parameters, go to the the General tab to view the parameters selection status.

Select Default Reservation Type on Sales Orders. Three reservation types are available in Microsoft Dynamics AX 2012:
- Manual
- Automatic
- Explosion

In Accounts receivable > Setup > Accounts receivable parameters, select the reservation type that is the default type when you create a new sales order. This value defaults into the sales order and the sales order line. If it is necessary, you can override the reservation setting manually in the sales order. Additionally you can override the sales order setting on the sales order line. For example, on a single sales order, you can have sales order lines with an Automatic reservation type and lines with Manual or Explosion settings.

Accounts receivable > Sales orders > All sales orders. Select the sales order record. Click Edit > Sales order tab > Header view > General tab.

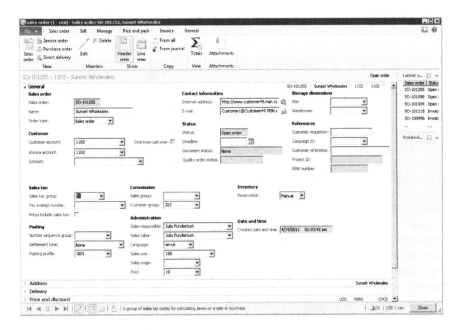

Accounts receivable > Sales orders > All sales orders. Select the sales order record. Click Edit > Sales order tab > Line view > Line details > Setup tab.

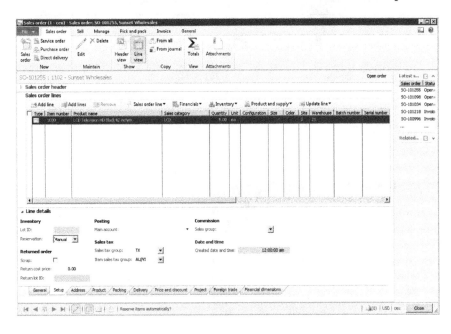

Marking

Marking resembles a reservation, and is used to connect receipt and issue transactions. Marking is based on the cost of an inventory receipt (lot) and is considered by inventory closing procedure. The financial value is based on the cost of the lot that is marked, not on inventory costing. This is important when you are assigning a specific item cost to an issue, and it is also helpful when you are returning items.

During inventory closing, marking overrules the item's inventory model setting, first in, first out (FIFO), last in, first out (LIFO), and other inventory models used to find the cost price for issues. Inventory closing always uses the cost price from the marked receipt.

Manual Reservations

You can use the Reservation form to make a manual reservation, and manually reserve an item from a sales order line.

To perform a manual reservation from a sales order line, open Accounts receivable > Common Forms > Sales orders > All sales orders, select an existing sales order or create a new sales order and sales order line and click Inventory > Reservation. The Reservation form appears.

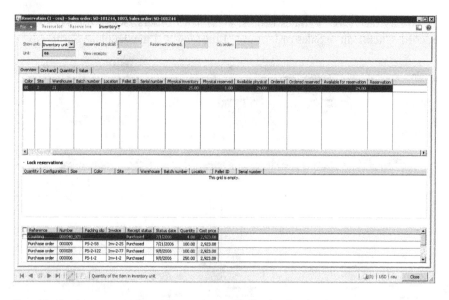

Specify the inventory dimensions that will display in the Reservation form by clicking from the Reservations form, Inventory > Dimensions display. Select the dimensions that will display and select the Save setup check box.

In the Reservation form, view the existing reservations in the following fields:
Physical reserved - Displays what physical inventory is reserved in the current lot of the selected sales order line.

Example: There is a sales order line for ten pieces, five of the ten pieces are reserved and "5" appears in the Reserved physical field.

Ordered reserved - Displays what ordered inventory is reserved for the current lot of the selected sales order line.

Ordered - Displays an un-reserved quantity of the lot of the selected sales order line.

Select - View receipts to view the receipt transactions for the current inventory dimension in a separate window at the bottom of the screen. Select this check box, for example, to view receipt dates for specific batches of on-hand inventory to reserve against the most recent batches, if this is an ordering priority.

In the Reservation field, enter the quantity to reserve[15].

User can view the changes in the Reservation form. The Physical reserved or Ordered reserved quantity is updated, depending on the available quantity on-hand and the setting for Inventory and warehouse management > Setup > Inventory and warehouse management parameters > General tab > Reserve ordered items.

Item Model Group

How Microsoft Dynamics AX 2012 responds when your try to reserve more than the available physical quantity for an item for a specific dimension depends on the item's item model group parameters:

- If the item has an item model group where Negative physical is selected, you can reserve more than the available inventory.
- If the item has an item model group where Negative physical is cleared, a warning is received stating that so many items cannot be reserved, and the reservation is canceled.

If the Reserve ordered items option is selected, the reservation can also consider ordered but not yet received quantities of goods for reservations.

An increase to the quantity on the sales order line does not increase the corresponding quantity reservation. The additional quantity receives the status On order, and the reservation to cover the additional quantity has to be performed manually.

If there is a decrease to the quantity on the sales order line, then the new quantity is less than the existing reservation. Microsoft Dynamics AX changes, and, or decreases the quantity accordingly.

---

[15] To automatically fill in the Reservation field for the current lot or the current inventory, click Reserve lot or Reserve line.

You can select the Reserve ordered items check box in the Inventory and warehouse management > Setup > Inventory and warehouse management parameters > General tab so that, reservations will be made against physically available quantities of the items, and items that are ordered but not yet received into the warehouse.

If this parameter is cleared, then reservations can only be made against physically available quantities of the item.

Note: The Reserve ordered items parameter works the same way for lines where the Reservation type is Automatic or Explosion.

Automatic Reservations

You can use the reservation type Automatic on a sales order line and the order quantity will be automatically reserved against the item's available on-hand inventory. If there is insufficient on-hand inventory, and the Reserved ordered items parameter is selected, Microsoft Dynamics AX 2012 will also make reservations against quantities of the item with the status Ordered.

A common scenario for automatic reservations is with items that have high sales volumes and are set up for automatic reservations. Because the items have high sales volumes, several orders can be taken within the same time period, with each order validated as having sufficient inventory on-hand to satisfy the order. However, at the time of picking, the demand for the items can exceed the inventory.

By using automatic reservations, deficits in inventory are visible at the time that the order line is created, instead of at the time of picking. By doing this, the order processor can inform the customer the item is out-of-stock or suggest other items. This improves customer service.

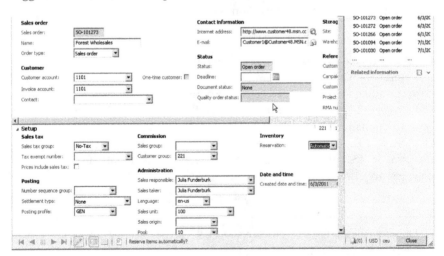

Automatic Reservation and Selection of Batch

Typically, automatic reservations are made on the oldest batch number. The oldest batch number is defined as the batch number with the lowest dimension values sorted in alphanumeric order.

The following figure shows how the batch numbers are selected as a diagram. The sales order line is for five pieces of a batch item. When the reservation type Automatic is used, batch A3 is automatically reserved against it, because it has the lowest alphanumeric identifier.

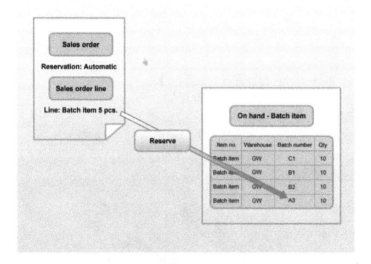

Date-Controlled and Backward From Ship Date

If you select Automatic reservation to create a sales order with a line and there is on-hand inventory to fill the order, the sales order automatically reserves the line quantity against the on-hand quantity.

However, if there is insufficient or no on-hand inventory for the item and the Reserve ordered items parameter is selected on the General tab of the Inventory and warehouse management > Setup > Inventory and warehouse management parameters form, Microsoft Dynamics AX 2012 will make reservations against the quantities of items that have the status Ordered.

If two or more receipts exist with different delivery dates, and both receipts have the same status of Ordered, that the sales order can be reserved against, the two parameters from item's Item Model Group named Date-controlled and Backward from ship date determine the receipt to reserve against. These parameters are selected on the Setup tab of the Inventory and warehouse management > Setup > Inventory > Item model groups form.

     - Date-controlled: Reservation occurs according to the FIFO principle. This means the complete sales order line quantity or the quantity that is unavailable as on-hand inventory, is reserved against the oldest purchase order with the status Ordered with the delivery date falling before the delivery date of the sales order line.

- Backward from ship date: Reservations are processed according to the LIFO principle. This means that the receipt with the most recent date is reserved.

Note: The Backward from ship date parameter cannot be selected from the delivery date parameter without first selecting the Date-controlled parameter.

Scenario: Date-Controlled Reservation
The next two diagrams explain graphically how reservation with these two parameters occurs.
In the Date-Controlled Reservation figure, no on-hand inventory is available and the reservation occurs against the earliest lot received before the sales order delivery date.

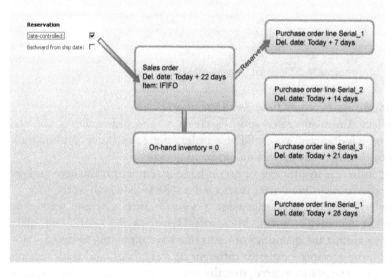

Scenario: Backward from Ship Date Reservation
In this figure, the scenario presented shows there is no available on-hand inventory. The sales order reserves against the last lot to be received before the sales order line delivery date, because the Backward from ship date parameter is selected.

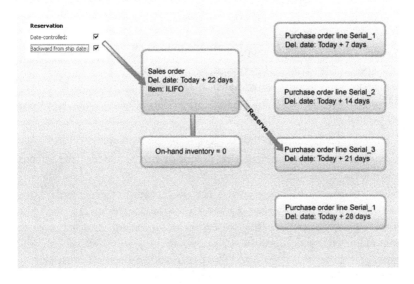

Inventory Dimensions, Primary Stocking and Reservations

The Warehouse dimension can be set up as Primary stocking by selecting the Primary stocking check box on the Storage dimension group form, or as non-primary stocking by leaving the check box cleared.

Primary Stocking and Reservations - Rule 1

When Primary stocking is specified for the warehouse, the reservation will be locked and cannot be changed manually. Regardless of whether the warehouse is specified as Primary stocking or not, if the warehouse is specified on the sales order line, automatic reservation only reserves items at this warehouse.

Primary Stocking and Reservations - Rule 2

When Primary stocking is not specified for the warehouse, and a dimension value is changed during physical receipt, the line is re-reserved and updated to the new value.

Procedure: Primary Stocking Inventory Dimensions and Reservation

This procedure explains how receiving the products at a warehouse other than the warehouse originally specified in the sales order line, and the warehouse is selected as Primary stocking, does not lead to an update of the warehouse dimension on the sales order line.

- Make sure that the Reserve ordered items parameter in Inventory and warehouse management > Setup > Inventory and warehouse management parameters > General tab is selected.
- Create a new product, and assign a Storage dimension group that has Primary stocking selected.
- Create a purchase order with two purchase order lines, and on each line specify a quantity of two pieces of the product. Both lines should have the same warehouse dimension selected.
- Manually create batch numbers and assign them to the purchase order lines.
- Create a sales order with the Reservation type Automatic on it.
- Create a sales order line for two pieces of the product. Only specify the warehouse dimension on the line.
- Click Inventory > Reservation. The Reservation form displays the sales order line is reserved against the purchase order line with the lowest batch number. The reservation is locked and cannot be manually changed because Primary stocking is selected on the Storage dimension group. The reservation record displays a corresponding record in the Lock reservations grid.
- In the Purchase order form on the purchase order line, register the arrival of the two pieces of the ordered product with the lowest batch number at another warehouse.
- Return to the sales order line and verify the reservation is updated. The Reservation form now displays the sales order is reserved against a batch number (the lowest available) that differs from the original batch number that is specified, but is still reserved at the same warehouse.

The reservation record displays a corresponding record in the Lock reservations grid.

Procedure: Non-primary Stocking Inventory Dimensions and Re-reservation
To show how not selecting Primary stocking for the warehouse affects the receipt for a product at a different warehouse and leads to a re-reservation on the sales order line, follow these steps.

- Create a new product, and assign a Storage dimension group that has Primary stocking cleared.
- Create a purchase order with two purchase order lines for the created product with a quantity of two on each line. The purchase order lines have the same warehouse specified on them and batch numbers attached.
- Create a sales order with Reservation type Automatic.

- Create a sales order line for the two pieces of the created product from a warehouse that differs from the warehouse specified on the purchase order lines.
- Click Inventory > Reservation. The Reservation form shows that a reservation is made between the sales order line and the purchase order line with the lowest batch number dimension. The reservation is not locked. The value in the Reservation field can be manually changed because Primary stocking is not selected on the product's Storage dimension group.
- In the purchase order, click Update line > Registration and register the arrival of the product.

Explosion Reservation

The Explosion reservation works according to the master planning item coverage setup. For example, when a requirement is far in the future, reserving the sales order line against a purchase order close to the current date, the system might reserve on-hand inventory for any orders that might be closer to the purchase order delivery date. Instead, master planning searches for a purchase order closer to the ship date for the sales order line. The number of days that master planning looks back is defined in the Positive days field located in the Master planning > Setup > Coverage > Coverage groups > General tab.

If master scheduling finds on-hand inventory which falls within the Positive days' time frame, a physical reservation is made between the sales order and the on-hand inventory. However, if no on-hand inventory is found within the Positive days' time frame, a planned purchase order is created and no reservation is made.

Example: On-hand Inventory Available Within Positive Days Limit

This figure shows how master planning can find on-hand inventory for the item within the five days Positive days' time frame specified in the coverage group. In this case the sales order line is reserved against the on-hand inventory.

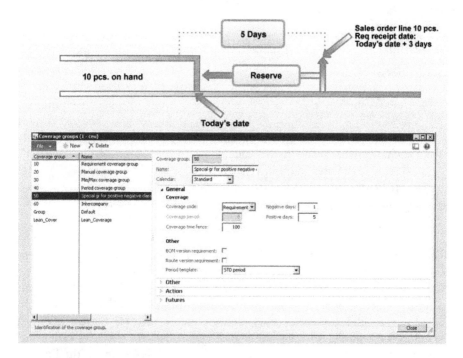

Example: On-hand Inventory Unavailable Within Positive Days Limit

This figure shows how master scheduling cannot find any on-hand inventory for the item within the five days Positive days' time frame. Therefore, a planned purchase order is created to fulfill the requirement.

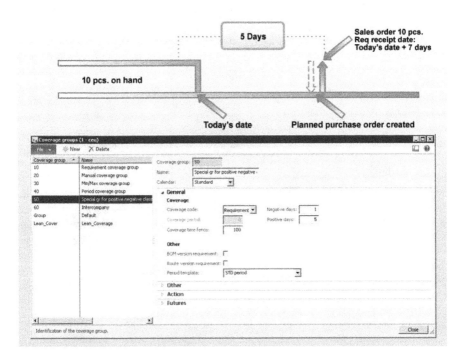

View Reservations

There are several ways to view reservations on items or orders. How to select the way to view the reservations depends on the information that you want. The reasons for viewing reservations include the following:

- Answer questions about available items.
- Inquire about delivery dates.
- View requirements for new purchases.
- View how items, on-hand or ordered, are reserved for various orders.

Viewing a Reservation on a Single Item can be done directly from the Items form through the On-hand form. The warehouse manager reviews on-hand inventory reservations for their top selling items. He or she uses this information to identify sales trends, and to make sure that there is sufficient inventory on-hand, in the correct location, for these items.

To view reservations on an item from the Item form, follow these steps:

- Open Product information management > Common Forms > Products > Released products.
- Select the item to view reservations for.

- Click Manage inventory > On-hand inventory to view reservations on various item dimensions. Selecting on-hand inventory displays information about the item's inventory-level status.
- Click the Overview tab to obtain a general overview for each selected inventory dimension and configuration.
- Click the On-hand tab to view additional information for each inventory dimension.

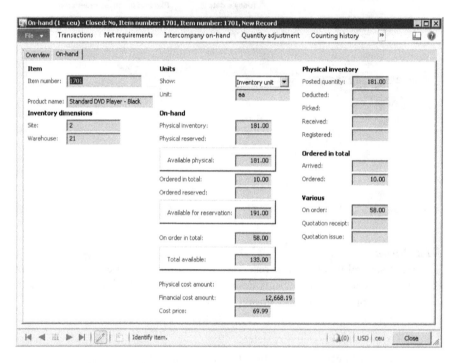

View Reservations from a Sales Order Line

From the sales order line, view all order reservations for the specific product dimension. The dimension the form displays reservations for is determined by the dimension opened from the Transactions on dimensions form.

For example, if opening the Transactions on dimensions form from a reservation where Warehouse 21 is specified, only transactions with Warehouse 21 attached to them are displayed.

Scenario: when the order processing clerks take a sales order, they are required to check on-hand inventory for the item being ordered. Because all reservations can be viewed from the sales order, the order processors can view all items at all stages in the sales cycle. By doing this, the order processors can guarantee their customers, that the item(s) the customer is ordering are available and can be shipped as promised.

To view Reservations on an Item from the Sales Order form, follow these steps:

- Open Accounts receivable > Common Forms > Sales Orders > All sales orders.
- Select the order and the sales order line to view reservations for.
- Click Inventory > Reservation to view reservations on various item dimensions.
- Select Inventory > On-hand transactions to view reservation details. The list shows the sales transactions that are reserved against the receipt transactions, such as purchases, for the dimension the form is opened from.

Lock Reservations

Use the Lock reservations feature to lock reservations on inventory dimensions where the inventory dimension does not have primary stocking selected in the storage dimension group that is attached to the product. This is useful if you want to reserve a specific product batch number for a specific sales order in the future.

To re-reserve a sales order line for a new inventory dimension, and for no future automatic reservations to be reserved against the batch, the locked reservation parameter is selected.

Clear the Lock Reservation Parameters

When sales order lines are manually reserved, the reservation system can also be set up so that the Lock reservation parameter does not prevent re-reservation of inventory.

This can be helpful in the situation where a manual reservation is made for a quantity of items with the status Ordered, but what is received is a quantity of the items with a different dimension value from what is originally reserved against.

By clearing the parameter for the dimension, the sales order line is re-reserved against the arrived quantity of the item.

Example: Clear the Lock Reservation Parameters

This procedure shows how clearing the Lock reservations parameter is used for re-reservation of inventory:

Make sure that the Reserve ordered items parameter is selected in Inventory and warehouse management > Setup > Inventory and warehouse management parameters.

- Use a new batch controlled item to create a purchase order for 20 pieces of an item. Do not bring this item in to inventory.

- Create a sales order for the 10 pieces of this item ordered by the customer, and manually reserve the quantity of 10 for the first batch number.
- In the Lock reservations pane, clear the Batch number parameter. Later that day, the Purchase Department registers the arrival of the second batch from the purchase order line by using the Inventory > Registration function.
- Review the sales order reservations for the item after some days, and notice that the reservation changed from the first batch on order to the second that is now registered.

This happened because of the removal of the Batch number Lock reservation parameter that activated the re-reservation of a quantity of arrived items instead of the batch the reservation is originally made against. If the Lock reservation parameter is still selected, re-reservation does not occur on the registering of the arrival of the second batch.

Cancel Reservations

Reservations can be canceled on items and orders. For example, reservations can be canceled if deliveries are unfulfilled or canceled, or if the items cannot be delivered on time. By canceling reservations in this situation, inventory is available for allocation to customers waiting for goods.

Reservations can also be canceled if existing reservations must be re-prioritized. For example, reservations can be canceled for smaller, lower priority orders to be able to deliver more important orders.

Scenario: The order processor creates a sales order for 50 pieces of the 1701 Standard DVD Player-Black for customer 2111 Rose Shopping Mall, for delivery in two weeks. A week later the Order Processor receives an order from Sunflower Shopping Mall, one of the company's most important customers, for 100 pieces of the 1701 Standard DVD Player-Black.

To make the reservation for this sales order line, the order processor must cancel the existing reservation with Rose Shopping Mall and then create a new reservation for Sunflower Shopping Mall for the 100 pieces of the on-hand inventory for the 1701 Standard DVD Player-Black.

Procedure: Cancel or Change a Reservation

To cancel or change a reservation, follow these steps:

- Open Accounts receivable > Common Forms > Sales Orders > All sales orders.
- Select the order for which the reservation should be changed and select the appropriate order line.
- Click Inventory > Reservation.

- To cancel the reservation, enter the quantity of zero in the Reservation field and then press Enter. The Physical reserved or Ordered reserved quantity is updated. Use this same procedure for both canceling and changing reservations on a single order.

Batch Reservations

Reservations can be manually changed on multiple orders at the same time. This is performed by accessing the Reservation form from the item's inventory transaction view.

These reservations can be changed independent of location, from a view of a single location, or on all locations.

Procedure: Change Reservations on Several Orders at the Same Time

To change reservations on several orders at the same time from a view of a specific location, follow these steps.

- Open Inventory and warehouse management > Inquiries > On hand.
- Select the item and location to change reservations on.
- Click Transactions to display a list of reservations for each order for the location. The list shows all purchase and sales orders for the item for each dimension.
- Click Inventory > Reservation.
- Enter the number of items to reserve for the dimension.

Note: Notice that when you close the Reservation form and return to the Transactions form, you might have to press F5, and then Restore, or reopen the Transactions form to update the totals.

Picking Reserved Items

In Microsoft Dynamics AX 2012, if an item to be picked is reserved, the system proposes the reserved lot, based on inventory dimensions. Use the Picking list registration form to override this proposal (see next chapter for more details regarding the picking process). This means that another inventory dimension can be proposed for the item.

This figure shows how reserving certain inventory dimension values means that they will be proposed when picking the sales order line.

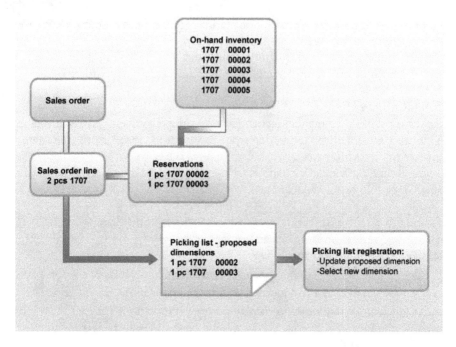

If user wants to reserve serialized inventory, Microsoft Dynamics AX 2012 proposes the reserved serial number during the picking process.
Prerequisites:

- Make sure that there are two pieces of item 1707 on-hand with serial numbers attached to them. Open Inventory and warehouse management > On-hand inventory.
- Verify the Serial number and Warehouse dimensions are selected in Accounts receivable > Setup > Forms > Form setup > Picking list and the Packing slip tabs. Make sure that the serial numbers are printed on picking list and packing slip updates.

Use the following steps:

1. Create a sales order for customer 2022 with one line sales order for two pieces of 1707 from Warehouse 21.

2. On the sales order line, click Inventory > Reservation. Manually reserve both of the serial numbers associated with 1707, by clicking Reserve lot. You may have to add Serial numbers to the display. Close the Reservation form.

3. Click Pick and pack > Picking list and select the Print picking list parameter to create a picking list for the items, and then click OK.

Notice the two serial numbers printed on the picking list are the two serial numbers previously reserved.

4. Click Pick and pack > Picking list registration. Notice that the serial numbers proposed are those previously reserved. You may have to add Serial numbers to the display.

5. On one of the lines, register the pick of another serial number by clicking the Serial number field in the Lines pane of the Picking list registration form and selecting another serial number.

6. Click Updates > Update all to register the pick of the serial numbers.

7. From the sales order lines, click Inventory > Transactions to view the serial number to which one of the lines it is updated to.

8. Click Pick and pack > Packing slip to create a packing slip update for the sales order. In the Quantity field, select Picked and select the Print packing slip field.

9. Click OK. Notice that the printed serial numbers match the serial numbers displayed in the step 7.

Note: If after Step 2 the item is picked by using the Inventory > Pick function, the serial number reserved for each line is still proposed in the Pick dialog box before the line is picked.

7 SALES ORDER PICKING

The picking process set up Microsoft Dynamics AX 2012 to help record the item number, configuration, quantity, and dimensions before recording a physical update.

Settings that affect how you perform the pick process include the following:

- Dimension groups – used to setup product, storage, and tracking dimensions requirements for picking.
- Item model group - Control the registration requirements.
- Accounts receivable setup parameters - Setup transactions for automatic picking.

Dimension Group

A product's dimension group determines the storage dimensions and tracking dimensions that can and must be recorded in the pick process. You open the Storage dimension groups form by clicking Product information management > Setup > Dimension groups > Storage dimension groups. You open the Tracking dimension groups form by clicking Product information management > Setup > Dimension groups > Tracking dimension groups.

In the following figure, the warehouse dimension, and location dimension are active. This means that they must be specified for products assigned to this Storage dimension group.

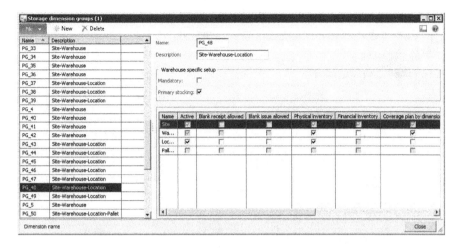

Item Model Group

The Item model group setup controls the product's picking requirements. The Item model group form is located at Inventory and warehouse management > Setup > Inventory > Item model groups. You can set up and maintain the settings for the Item model group on the Setup tab of the Item model group. The fields in the Physical update field group determine the workflow used when you send or receive items. With these fields, you can set rules on how an order is handled for receiving and shipping.

When shipping an item, you can use three parameters in the Setup tab of the Item model group form:

- Picking requirements: This parameter determines whether the item's inventory records must have the status Picked before a packing slip can be physically updated or before an inventory journal can be posted. When this is selected, the picking list registration must be manually posted.

- Deduction requirements: This parameter determines that you must physically update item deductions before they can be financially updated.

- Consolidated picking method: This parameter determines that you manage item picking through a consolidated picking output order type with the pick of multiple orders, and by using picking areas and shipment functionality. Therefore, make sure that this check box is cleared when you register a pick from the sales order line.

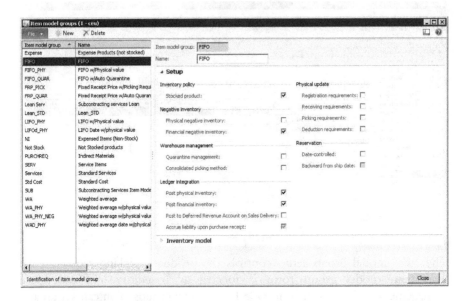

Accounts Receivable Setup

In the Accounts receivable parameters, you can set up transactions for automatic picking at the release to picking point in time. The Accounts receivable parameters form is located at Accounts receivable > Setup > Parameters.

Note: If both Picking requirements is selected in the item model group and Picking route status is set to Completed in the Accounts receivable parameters, the Accounts receivable parameters overrules the settings in the Item model group. This means that the picking list registration is performed automatically.

Picking process

The picking process can be setup in three ways:

- Automatic - Used when a response to the picking list is not necessary, for example, when the items sold are always in stock, or when users do not have to specify different dimension values, than what is on the sales order line or what is reserved.
- Manual - one step process - Use this process if you want to enter the dimensions and register the pick from the sales order line.
- Manual – two steps process - Use when you want to assign a picking task and then perform a physical pick.

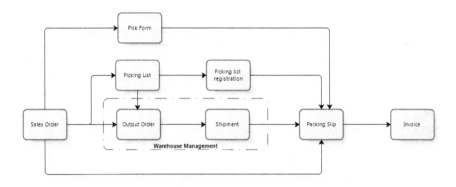

Release Sales Order Picking

The Release sales order picking functionality helps warehouse employees gain an overview of the sales orders that are to be released for picking, based on actual availability of items and considering customer service priority. By using this platform for the picking process, you are ensured that only picking lists for items in stock are created.

There are two forms to make the picking process easier: Release sales order picking for sales orders and Release transfer order picking for transfer orders.

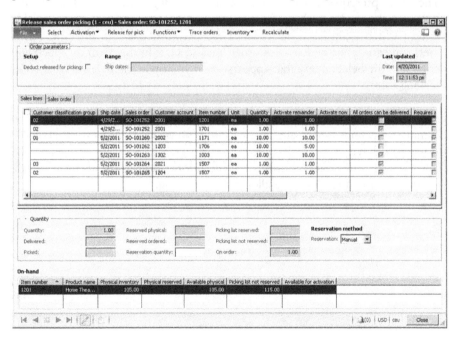

Customer Classification Groups

You can use customer classification groups to flag customers according to service priority. If back orders exist for sales order lines, one of the criteria that you can use to determine which sales orders must have quantity available allocated to them is the customer classification group that you attach to the customer for the line.

The sales manager must be able to determine which customers' back orders must be on-hand in inventory to allocate to them first. To create a priority ranking, the warehouse manager attaches a customer classification group to the customers. The warehouse manager creates premium and standard classifications, 1 and 2 that are then attached to customers.

Later, the warehouse manager must allocate available inventory to two sales order lines with the same inventory dimensions specified for them on the same shipping date. One sales order line is for a customer whose classification group is 1, and one line is for a customer whose classification group is 2.
Because classification 1 customers take priority, all the quantity that is available is allocated to the classification 1 customer's line.

Set Up the Release Sales Order Picking Form

The basic prerequisite for viewing and processing sales order lines in the Release sales order picking form is that there is some quantity available against which to, at least partly, fulfill the sales order line. If this criterion is met, you can define which sales order lines to view in the form by specifying criteria in the Select query that appears when you open the Release sales order picking form.

Additionally, by using the Deduct released for picking option, you can eliminate any lines for picking where there is no available quantity to allocate. When you have selected the sales order lines that you want viewed in the Release sales order picking form, use the information in the form to decide about the on-hand items to be allocated for picking.

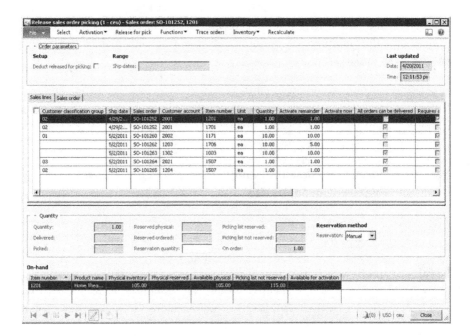

Quantity Field Group
Use the Quantity field group to obtain a detailed breakdown of the quantity status for the current sales order line. View information for the quantity of the order line that has already been picked or reserved and if reservations exist on ordered, but not yet received receipts.

The Picking list reserved and Picking list not reserved fields are useful to the warehouse manager who is trying to allocate on-hand inventory:

- Picking list reserved: Shows quantities of the item for the current sales order line that are updated with a picking list and reserved. The reservation will prevent these items from being allocated for another sales order.
- Picking list not reserved: Shows quantities of the item for the sales order line that have a picking list printed for them but have not yet been reserved in the process. Therefore, although the items are still available for allocation elsewhere, they are allocated for this order's pick. By considering this field when allocating inventory to sales orders, you can make sure that you do not allocate on-hand items that are picking list updated, but not reserved, for another sales order.

On-hand Field Group
The On-hand field group resembles the Quantity field group except it displays values for all on-hand items throughout the system. The field group

shows different quantities of on-hand items available for each inventory dimension and their status of physical inventory, physical reservation, physical availability, the number of picking list non-reserved items, and other categories of availability.

Allocate On-hand Inventory for Sales Order lines

When you have defined exactly which sales order lines that you want to view in the Release sales order picking form, you are ready to start allocating on-hand inventory to the order lines.

Allocate on-hand inventory for sales order lines individually by entering a quantity in the Activate now field on the sales order line or by selecting one of the activation methods from Activation.

Checkboxes in the Sales Line Tab

The check boxes in the Sales line tab of the Release sales order picking form are system selected and provide information about to what extent orders can be fulfilled and how to fulfill them. The check boxes are described below:

- All orders can be delivered - Indicates whether all orders with the same item number and inventory dimensions (storage location) can be delivered by using the current on-hand inventory.
- Requires allocation - Select if you have to decide about how on-hand items must be allocated to the sales order. For example, if you have to allocate on-hand items to two sales order lines where there is insufficient inventory to fulfill both, the check box is selected and the warehouse manager must make an allocation decision.
- Production order exists - Select if there is a production order line that needs the same item with the same inventory dimension with an estimated date before or equal to the shipment date entered in the Select dialog box.
- Transfer order exists - Select if there is a transfer order line that needs the same item with the same inventory dimension with an estimated date before or equal to the shipment date entered in the Select dialog box.
- Possible delivery percentage - The percent is calculated on the number of sales order lines that can be fulfilled for a sales order. For example, if two out of the three sales order lines for a sales order can be filled, then the Possible delivery percentage is 67 percent.

Select Criteria for displaying Sales Order Lines

When you open the Release sales order picking by clicking Inventory and warehouse management > Periodic > Release sales order picking, you define which data to display in the form by entering selection criteria in the Select query.

Use the selection criteria to:

- Only show the release sales order lines that will be shipped before next week.

  For example: Order Lines.Ship Date = (LessThanDate(7))

- Sort sales order lines by the top customer classification group for the relevant customer so that you can prioritize the allocation of limited on-hand orders to back orders for high priority customers.

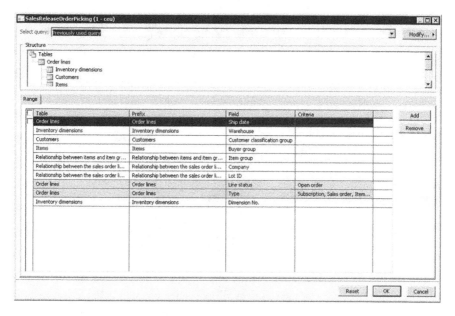

Deduct Released for Picking

The Deduct released for picking check box on the Release sales order picking form addresses the problem that some companies experience when they create picking lists without reserving items for the picking list. If you picking list update a sales order line without reserving the items on the line, it could appear that these items are available for use in another order, even though the items are designated for the original order by their inclusion in the picking list for the original order.

By selecting the Deduct released for picking check box, you make sure any order lines that are picking list updated, but not reserved, are eliminated from the Release sales order picking form.

Therefore, Deduct released for picking is used by order takers to obtain a clearer understanding of whether they can allocate on-hand items for a sales order line.

You can also be in the situation where a quantity of available items, but not the whole quantity, is picking list updated without being reserved at the same time. In this situation you can see the amount that was picking list updated but not reserved in the Picking list not reserved field in the On-hand Pane of the form.

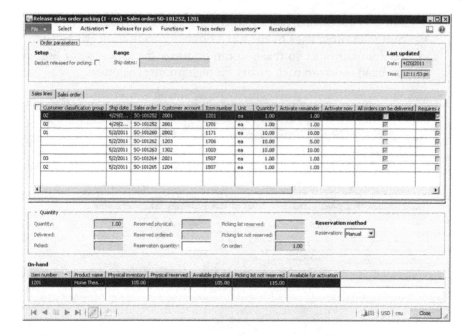

Deliver Remainder

Use the Deliver remainder feature to close back orders if, for example, you have insufficient on-hand quantity to fill the sales order but have established that it is acceptable to the customer to whom you make an under delivery. The feature works in a similar manner to how it does in the Sales order form. To open the Update remaining quantity form from the Released sales order picking form, click Functions > Deliver remainder.

Automatic Registration of a Pick

You can set up a pick to be automatically registered by selecting Completed in the Picking route status parameter in the Accounts receivable parameters form.

Automatic registration of a pick means that a sales order can continue to the Packing slip update after you post the Picking list because the Picking list registration step is automatically completed.

Manual Registration of a Pick

Items that require a manual documentation of dimension values, such as serial or batch numbers follow a one-step or two-step picking process.

- The manual one-step process: You can only perform this process from the Sales order. From the sales order line, you enter the Pick form, where you can enter the dimension values and pick the products.
- The manual two-step process: You can use this process to assign a picking task and then perform the physical pick. The process involves:
  - Posting and printing a picking list of items to be picked in the warehouse.
  - Registering the actual dimension values and posting the pick.

Item Pick Registration of Serialized and Batch Inventory

Serial and batch numbers are inventory tracking dimensions and can only be allocated to items, where the tracking dimension group allows for it. When the dimension values Serial number and Batch number are activated, you must specify them when picking, unless Blank issue allowed is activated for the dimension. When the Blank issue allowed check box is selected, it prevents the specification of the dimension when the physical issues are updated.

Edit, Reverse and Split a Pick

During the picking process, you can work with a transaction in the Pick form. To activate the attribution of various Inventory dimension values, a picked line can be:

- Reversed
- Edited
- Split

To update a pick on a sales line, you must first reverse the transaction.

Note: To reverse a pick, the Issue status of the sales line must not be Delivered. When a Packing slip is posted, the transaction is closed and it cannot be reversed.

Confirm Inventory Storage Dimensions after Pick Registration

At Contoso Entertainment Systems, some inventory storage dimensions are not confirmed until after pick registration. The active inventory dimensions at Contoso Entertainment Systems are as follows:

- Serial number
- Batch number
- Warehouse
- Site

For some items, because there is so much stock on-hand within the warehouses, the storage dimensions of the items that will be picked are not known until the pick is completed.

Microsoft Dynamics AX 2012 supports editing, reversing, and splitting of picks. By doing this, the company can make the changes to the storage dimensions after picking, based on the results of the pick.

Split a Pick

Use the split function when items on one sales order line must be divided, for example, when:

- Picking both serial and batch numbers.
- Picking lines from several warehouses.

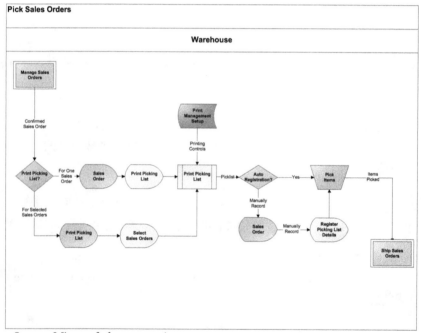

Source: Microsoft documentation

8 CUSTOMER RETURNS

One of the other aspects involved with sales order processing is item returned processing from customers. A customer may return items and claim for replacement and/or a financial compensation and may determine the selling company, depending on the evaluation of the service department, to apply a disposition code such as credit only, credit and scrap, replace and credit or replace and scrap, which will determine the subsequent steps in the processing flow. Customers can return items to a company for various reasons, such as an item is defective, or an item does not fulfill the customer's expectations.

The return process starts with a request from a customer to return an item, and progresses to creating a return order in Microsoft Dynamics® AX 2012.

The customer returns scenarios cover how to create, confirm the arrival of returned items, and inspect the returned items. The final two scenarios show the final procedures of processing the sales order and updating the return order.

Return Material Authorization (RMA) processing builds on sales order functionality. Each RMA has an associated sales order, termed the Return order, and an optional second sales order, termed the Replacement order. Both sales orders have the same order number, but use a different order type, and both orders link to the originating RMA number.

Return Order

Every RMA includes an associated sales order (with a sales order type of returned order) that only handles the arrival, receipt, and credit note for the returned item. When you create a RMA it automatically creates the associated return order that represents a mirror image of the RMA. Any changes that you make to the RMA information automatically changes information in the return order.

Replacement Order

An RMA can include a second associated sales order when a replacement order must be shipped to the customer. You can manually create the replacement order for the RMA to support immediate shipment, or automatically create the replacement order after the RMA line item (with a disposition code that indicates replacement) undergoes arrival/inspection and receipt.

The replacement order has the same functionality that is associated with a sales order. For example, you can use it to configure a custom product as the replacement item, create a production order to repair a returned item, create a direct delivery purchase order for sending the replacement from a vendor, or support other purposes.

Customer Returns

A customer contacts the Customer Service Representative, because there are some problems with the latest order the customer received, meaning some delivered items are defective, and one item did not meet the customer's needs. The customer service representative finds the reference number of the order and creates new return orders for the customer. By using the reference number, he finds the customer invoice and views the ordered items. The customer explains the following:

- Item A was damaged during shipment
- Item B does not function
- Item C is not intact
- Item D is unwanted - the customer wanted another color

The employee validates and selects the various items one by one from the customer invoice he found. In support of the later inspection or troubleshooting process, he enters the expected return quantity, Estimated Time of Arrival (ETA) for the items, a reason code[16], and any additional information the customer provided.

Employee informs the customer of the deadline for returning the items and the address of the warehouse. Finally, he sends the return order document in paper or electronic form to the customer. The return order document contains the Return Materials Authorization (RMA) number that identifies the return order and authorizes the customer to return goods to the company.

---

[16] The Reason code is a return order header property. In the above example, it means that employee must create four return orders, one for each item, and has to enter one reason code for each item return.

Scenario: Receive the Returned Items

Ten days pass, and the responsible for shipping and receiving receives the returned items at the return warehouse. He views the accompanying return order documents, evaluates the returned items, and counts and checks them against the return orders.

After that he opens the Arrival overview form, finds the arrival among the other returns, and creates a new item arrival journal. Because of the imposed requirement for inspection, he specifies that the item must be inspected[17] for each journal line. He then posts the arrival journal.

If the company policy permitted the shipping and receiving manager to make decisions on how to dispose of the returned items, he could have applied a disposition code to the journal line instead of sending the item(s) to inspection.

Confirm the Arrival of Returned Items

The Customer Service Representative is notified that the returned items have arrived. He mails the customer a confirmation that the returned items have arrived at the return warehouse and additional investigations will begin.

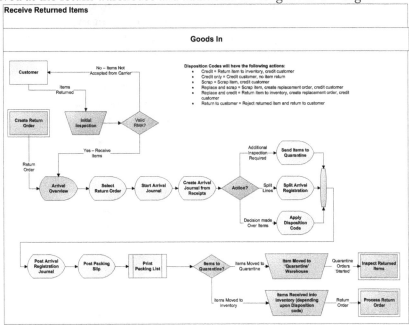

Source: Microsoft documentation

---

[17] Inspection means that the items will pass through quarantine orders and to the quarantine warehouse.

Inspect the Returned Items in Quarantine

The Quality Controller has received four quarantine orders and the returned items, and now starts to inspect them. He examines the described symptoms and descriptions to make sure that those are correct.

When the inspection is complete, he updates the quarantine orders with the following information:

- Item A is not functioning. It receives disposition code "61-Scrap item, credit customer" with the disposition action: Scrap. The customer will be credited and the item will be scrapped.

- Item B is delivered with the wrong antenna. It receives disposition code "31 - Replace item, credit customer" with the disposition action: Replace and credit. The Quality Controller or the Customer Service Representative, will specify a replacement item. The customer will be credited, and a replacement item will be entered on a new sales order.

- Item C must be repaired. It receives disposition code "51" with the disposition action: Return to customer. The item will be repaired and eventually returned to the customer. The customer will be invoiced for charges, and parts according to company policy.

- Item D is working fine, and it is returned to inventory. It receives disposition code "11 - Put item back in to inventory, credit customer who has disposition action: Credit. The customer will be credited and the item will be put into inventory again.

The Quality controller cannot end the quarantine order for item C, until it is repaired, but the remaining three quarantine orders can be ended. Ending the orders will transfer the information about disposition codes back to the return order lines. This makes them available for additional processing by the Order Processor.

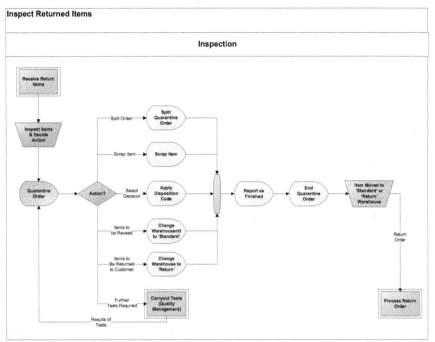

Source: Microsoft documentation

Process the Return Order
The Order Processor packing slip updates the return orders to receive the returned items into inventory, and to create replacement orders if they are required. Item C is through inspection, and is repaired and ready to be shipped back to the customer. The Quality Controller can end the quarantine order. Now the Order Processor can return the repaired item to the customer, and then close the return order.

Set Up Customer Returns
Returns can be categorized according to return reasons or methods of disposition, and specific charges can be combined with the various return categories.

Return Reason Codes
Applying reason codes on returns can help simplify the analysis of return patterns. The reason codes are set up to determine why a customer wants to return item(s). Some companies have many reason codes, and they will group the reason codes in Reason code groups for a better overview and for accumulated reporting.

To set up return reason code groups, open the Return reason code groups form from Sales and marketing> Setup > Sales orders > Returns > Return reason code groups, click New to create a new reason code, specify the name of the return reason code group and enter a description and close the form.

To create a return reason code, open the Return reason code form from Sales and marketing > Setup > Sales orders > Returns > Return reason codes or from the Return reason code groups form, by clicking Return reason codes; click New to create a new reason code; enter the name of the reason code and a description; from the Return reason code group field, select the return reason code group to link to the reason code. Charges can also be specified on the reason code, and added to the return order when the reason code is applied; close the form.

The reason codes are applied in the Return order form header.

Disposition Codes

Disposition codes are also a part of the customer returns setup. They determine what will happen to the returned items from a physical and a financial perspective. The available options are defined by the disposition actions.

As part of the item arrival and inspection, a disposition code will be assigned to the returned goods.

In addition to determining how to dispose of the returned goods, disposition codes can cause charges to be applied to the return line and they can also be used to group returns for statistical analysis.

Disposition code	Action	Description
11	Credit	Put item back into inventory, credit customer
12	Credit	Repair and add to inventory, credit customer
21	Credit only	Credit, no return of item
31	Replace and credit	Replace item, credit customer
41	Replace and scrap	Replace item, scrap returned, credit customer
51	Return to customer	Reject returned item, return to customer.
61	Scrap	Scrap item, credit customer

Identification of the disposition code.

A disposition code can be applied when you perform the following tasks:
- Create the return order.
- Register item arrival.
- End a quarantine order.

Disposition Actions

Microsoft Dynamics AX 2012 has six predefined disposition actions that define the combination of the following:
- The physical handling of the returned item.
- The financial effect of the return transaction.
- If a replacement item must be sent to the customer.

The Disposition actions are:
- Credit - Return the item to inventory, then credit the customer.
- Credit only - Credit the customer without requiring or expecting the item to be returned. The Credit only disposition action is available from the Return order form only, as part of when you create the return order.
- Scrap - Scrap the item, credit the customer.
- Replace and scrap - Scrap the item, create a replacement order, and credit the customer.
- Replace and credit - Return the item to inventory, create a replacement order, and then credit the customer.
- Return to customer - Reject the returned item, and return it to the customer.

Create a Disposition Code

To create a disposition code, open the Disposition codes form from Sales and marketing > Setup > Sales orders > Returns > Disposition codes; click New to Create a new disposition code; type the name for the disposition code and the description; select an action for the disposition code in the Action field; close the Disposition codes form.

Return Charges

Many companies want customers to pay a return fee or special return handling charges.

In Microsoft Dynamics AX 2012 you can set up charges as a standard fee based on a return reason code or disposition code, or you can add them manually to the order header or lines. For example, company can setup reason codes and disposition codes for charges, e.g. 15 percent handling fee or for item repaired 10 percent repair charge.

You can set up charges for reason codes by clicking Charges in the Reason codes form.

For the disposition codes, you can set up charges by clicking Charges in the Disposition code form.

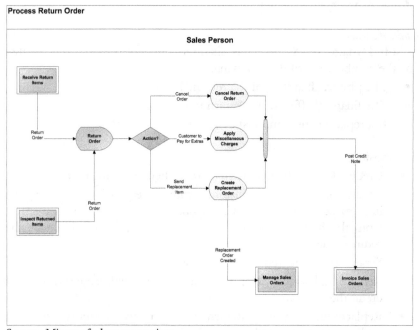

Source: Microsoft documentation

Returns and Intercompany

Returns in Microsoft Dynamics AX 2012 also support intercompany direct returns.

In an intercompany setup, a user can have one company engaging directly with the end customer, and the sister company or subsidiary in the intercompany chain receiving the actual return order.

The created intercompany order chain resembles a standard direct delivery order, where the actual processing of the chain takes advantage of the Returns feature.

Handling Customer Returns from a Sister Company - When the customer represents a sister company, the creation of the RMA (and its associated sales order for the returned item) will automatically create an intercompany purchase order within the database for the sister company. A second intercompany purchase order is also generated when you create a replacement order for the RMA. The RMA number is identified on both intercompany purchase orders.

Handling Replacement Orders that involve Purchases from a Sister Company
A replacement order line item can involve a purchase from a vendor that represents a sister company, such as a direct delivery purchase order for sending the replacement item to the customer. The creation of the purchase order automatically creates an intercompany sales order within the database for the sister company (identified with the RMA number).

When you create intercompany return orders, the default behavior is for the system to assign the same (RMA) number to the intercompany return order that is assigned to the original return order. This implies a risk for a conflict if the RMA number is already being used in the intercompany company ("Company B"). To avoid this situation, the number sequence for return order numbers must be set up according to the following rule:
If two or more companies participate in an intercompany relationship with one another, they must set up different number series for return orders, for example:
In Company A: "RMA_A_#####"
In Company B: "RMA_B_#####"
Then, automatic assignment and synchronization of return order numbers will work.

Create a Return Order
The return order resembles a sales order and is characterized by a status that indicates what is processed on the return order. On the return order, there is a header Status field, with values as following:

- Created - Upon creation, the header status will be Created. This indicates that this is a planned return order. The status on a return order line is Expected. The order can be deleted or canceled, and a user can create new lines on a return order with a status of Created.

- Open - When the first item starts to arrive in inventory, the status of the return order is changed to Open. The status on a return order line can be one of the following: Expected, Registered, Received, Quarantine, or Invoiced. A user cannot create new lines on a return order with status Open.

- Invoiced - When a return order is fully credited (all lines are invoice updated) the status will change to Invoiced, and the order cannot be opened again for additional processing. The status on a return order line is Invoiced. A user cannot create new lines on a return order with a status of Invoiced.

- Canceled - If the customer forgets to return an item, or if items never appear in a given time frame, a return order can be canceled. The user can delete the return order, as long as a historical record is not needed, instead of canceling it. The status on a return order line is Canceled. A user cannot create new lines on a return order with the status of Canceled.

Return Order Form

The Return order form has two views available: header view and line view. These resemble the Sales order form.

When you open the Return order form, by default, the form will always open in the Line view. The line view version of the form has three fast tabs:

- Return order header: Displays basic information from the header of the return order which applies to all lines of the return order. However, some fields can be overridden at line level.
- Return order lines: Displays a list of each item or service for the return order.
- Line details: Displays additional information for the line that is selected in the Return order lines tab. The additional information on the Line details tab is split into several tabs across the bottom of the tab page which divides the additional fields into logical groups or areas.

To enter detailed information about a return order into the header and optionally have the information copied to all the lines of the return order, you must open the Header view. To access the Header view, click Header view in the Show group of the Action Pane on the Return order form.

When in the Header view of the return order form, the Header view button on the Action Pane will be highlighted to give you a visual indication of the current view.

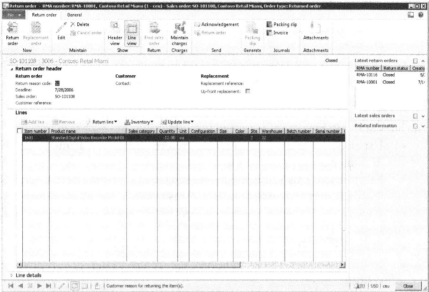

Return Order Form - Action Pane

The options available in the Action Pane when in Header View are:

- Maintain charges - Add or modify charges for the return order such as restocking fees or repair costs.
- Find sales order - Create a return order by retrieving the information from the original sales order, and the sales order lines. A return order is not required to be matched against a sales order.
- Cancel order - Cancel the return order.
- Send acknowledgement - Send an acknowledgement document to the customer to confirm the returned items have arrived at the warehouse.
- Send return order - Send the return order document to the customer.
- Create replacement order - Create an up-front replacement order for the items that will be returned. This function lets you send replacement items to the customer before the defective items are returned. This helps when a customer, for example, must have the spare parts available before he or she can dismantle the defective item. The up-front replacement order is an alternative to the replacement order created when you apply a disposition code when the returned item is inspected and it is used as a way to increase customer satisfaction.
- Packing slip - Packing slip update the return order.

On the Lines Action Pane in the Return order form, the following options are available:

- Charges can be created for each line. Click Return line > Maintain charges.
- A user can find a replacement item if the disposition code specifies replacement. Click Return line > Replacement item.

Return Order Form Line Status
The lines in the Return order form can have the following statuses:.

- Expected - On a created or open return order, this status indicates nothing has happened to the return order line.
- Registered - This status indicates items are posted in the item arrival journal, upon item arrival, or when it is returned from quarantine.
- Received - This status indicates items are packing slip updated and received in inventory.
- Quarantine - This status indicates items are currently in quarantine.
- Invoiced - This status indicates the return order line is invoice credited.
- Canceled - This status indicates the return order line is canceled.

To create a return order, open the Return orders form from Sales and marketing >Common > Return orders > All return orders, click Return order located in the New grouping of the Return order Action Pane. Select the customer account in the Customer account field, optionally specify a customer contact person in the Contact field, click General and select a Return reason code for returning the items, and then click OK. From the Action Pane Return group, click Find sales order to open the Find sales order form. Select the Mark check box on the line to be returned and update the Quantity to return field, if it is necessary. Or, if you do not want to associate the Return order with a sale order, you can select an item number in the Lines section of the Return order form.

Note: The system prevents you from registering a customer return that is greater than the quantity that is sold to the customer, if the return order is matched against the Sales order.

Microsoft Dynamics AX 2012 automatically fills in a return warehouse and expected deadline for returning the items. The deadline is calculated based on the setup of the Period of validity parameter, located on the General tab in the Accounts receivable parameters form.
The status of the return order is Created, and because the items have not arrived in inventory, there will be no inventory transactions for the return order yet. However, there is a parameter named Allow reservation located in the Line details section on the General tab of the Return order form. You can

use the Allow reservation check box to trigger the immediate generation of inventory transactions, if returned goods are known to be in perfect condition. This causes the incoming goods to become visible in the inventory and warehouse system, that makes them available to fulfill demand from other sales orders.

Best practices

Although only one warehouse and one delivery address can be selected on the Return order header, you can assign each return item line to a different warehouse (and address). If the customer sends the returned goods to the warehouse address quoted on the header, all lines in the Arrival overview form might not be visible to the receiving warehouse, if that location is filtering to view returns assigned to its warehouse only.

To avoid this, assign all return lines to the same warehouse that is specified in the header. If you cannot do that, because some items are set up with a mandatory sales warehouse, then create a separate return order for each item and assign it to the appropriate warehouse in the return order header.

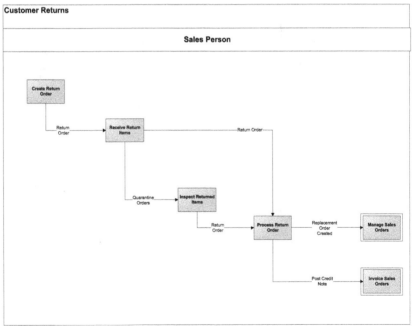

Source: Microsoft documentation

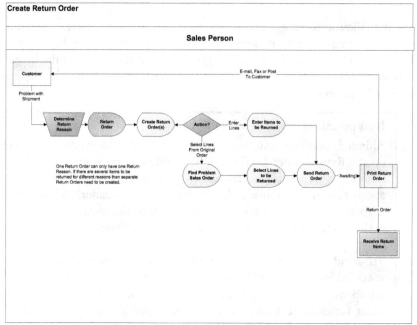

Source: Microsoft documentation

9 PACKING SLIP AND INVOICING

Packing slip and Invoicing update of a sales order (or in some scenarios several sales orders simultaneously) are the last steps in sales order processing. You are free to post the sales order invoice with or without separate packing slip posting (in AX terminology a packing slip[18] for a sales is a delivery note document). The invoice increases the open customer balance on the one hand and reduces the inventory value on the other hand. The packing slip and invoicing updates can be done for the complete order or it may be partial invoicing of the sales order. After invoicing all lines of a sales order entirely, the sales order is completed.

Payment for the invoice is a separate process in finance, and some of the details will be presented in the next chapter.

If you want to invoice items, you need to select a sales order that you ship and invoice.

If you want to post invoices not referring to item records, you may use free text invoices. In the lines of a free text invoice, you need to enter ledger numbers instead of item numbers. Such an invoice has no connection to items and therefore no impact on inventory and supply chain management.

Sales Order Packing slip update
When the item is ready to ship to the customer, you will post a packing slip. When you have posted the packing slip, the system recognizes that the sales order demand is satisfied and reduces the physical on-hand inventory, if you have not performed the Picking list registration. If Picking list registration is

---

[18] If ledger integration is activated for the packing slip receipt, Dynamics AX will post transactions in the general ledger in parallel to the inventory transactions. These ledger transactions will reverse when you post the related invoice.

performed, it is at that time that the system will reduce the physical on-hand inventory.

To generate a sales order packing slip, open Sales and marketing > Common > Sales orders > All sales order, select the sales order to generate the packing slip, in the Pick and pack tab of the Action Pane, click Packing slip in the Generate group. The Packing slip posting form opens (for a description of the Packing Slip posting form go to the *Generate a Sales Order Packing Slip* Section in the chapter 5 Sales orders). In the Posting packing slip form, in the Quantity field, select the All option. Select the Print packing slip check box to print the packing slip. Click OK on the Posting dialog box.

If the quantities on the packing slip update equal the ordered quantities, the value in the sales order Status field changes to Delivered. If there is a back order on one or more items, the sales order status remains as Open order.

Cancel a Packing Slip

It may be the case when a packing slip was wrong and it needs to be cancelled or corrected. Canceling the packing slip[19] reverses all packing slip posting and returns the product to inventory, if it is a stocked product. The Packing slip journals form displays all generated packing slips. From this form, you can correct or cancel the packing slip, if the packing slip was generated incorrectly or by accident.

To cancel a packing slip open Sales and marketing > Common > Sales orders > All sales order, select the sales order for which to cancel the packing slip and in the Pick and pack tab on the Action Pane, click Packing slip in the Journals group. Select the packing slip that you want to cancel and then click Cancel. Click OK in the dialog box and close the infolog, then close the Packing slip journal form.

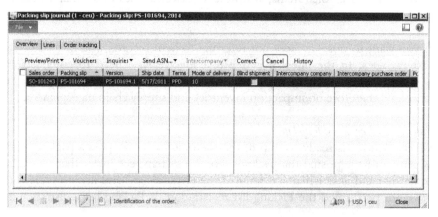

---

[19] A packing slip cannot be canceled or corrected if the sales order is invoiced.

Correcting a packing slip

To correct a packing slip, open Sales and marketing > Common > Sales orders > All sales order, select the sales order, for which to cancel the packing slip. In the Pick and pack tab on the Action Pane, click Packing slip in the Journals group and select the packing slip that you want to correct and then click Correct.

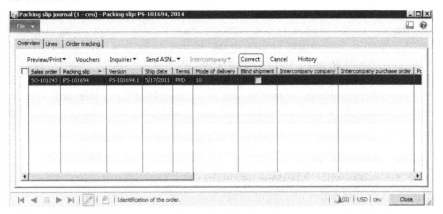

In the Correct packing slip form, make any necessary corrections or changes to the packing slip, then click OK and close the Packing slip journal form.

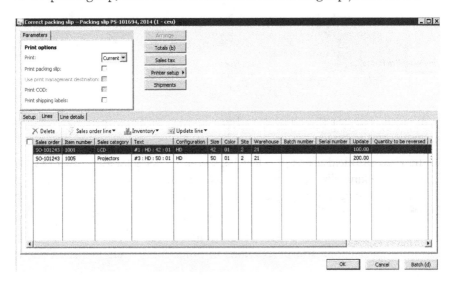

View changes between Packing Slip Versions

All changes on each packing slip version are traced. You can view all changes to a given packing slip on the Compare packing slip versions form.

To access this form, open Packing slip journal from the Sales order form, or open Sales and marketing > Inquiries > Journals > Packing slip, click History to open the Packing slip history form to show the multiple versions, then click Compare versions. From the Compare packing slip versions form, you can view and compare the differences of each packing slip version.

In order to see the inventory transactions after packing slip posting, you may use the button Inventory/Transactions in the order line concerned. After posting a packing slip, the issue status of the inventory transaction is "Deducted". The posting date of the packing slip shows in the column Physical date of the inventory transaction, the Financial date will remain empty until you post the invoice. If you want to know the packing slip number, you may switch to the tab Update.

Sales Order Invoice update

After the sales order has now been shipped, the next process step is to invoice the sales order using generate invoice[20].

To invoice update a sales order, navigate to Sales and marketing > Common > Sales orders > All sales orders, select the desired sales order and in action pane switch to the Invoice tab, then click Invoice within Generate group.

In Invoice form set the check box Print invoice to True, then click OK to generate print to screen.

In the Quantity field user can select Packing Slip, if he wants to post exactly what was packing slip updated (if the case, he may select individual packing slips for invoicing pushing the button Select packing slip when choosing "Packing Slip"), or All to post all un-invoiced quantities from the sales order.

Posting the invoice posts general ledger transactions, inventory transactions, customer transactions and transactions in other sub-ledgers like sales tax, if

---

[20] Accounts receivables>Periodic>Sales update>invoice can be used as an alternative. This allow for a centralized and consolidated view on sales order line shipped awaiting to be invoiced.

applicable. If all lines are invoiced completely, the order status will change to "Invoiced".

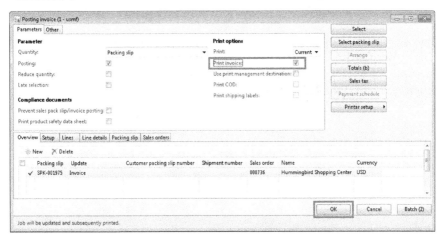

Free Text Invoices

If you want to post invoices not referring to item records, you may use free text invoices. In the lines of a free text invoice, you need to enter ledger numbers instead of item numbers. Such an invoice has no connection to items and therefore no impact on inventory and supply chain management. Several improvements were made in Microsoft Dynamics AX 2012 regarding free text invoices, giving users the possibility to add quantities and unit price, sub ledger distribution is supported to give users the flexibility to distribute revenue across multiple ledger accounts, recurring invoice templates let users easily create recurring invoices, streamlining the invoice process and avoiding the need to manually create monthly invoices. In the past, invoice correction has been a manual and difficult task. Now Microsoft Dynamics AX 2012 supports creating a correcting invoice that can be routed through workflow for approval. The correction functionality automatically creates the necessary transactions and audit trail.

Susan (Sales clerk) takes orders from clients and from other sales agents who purchase products and services. Susan must to be able to add quantity and price information to free text invoices for service charges. In the following scenario, Susan creates a free text invoice to charge the customer for installation and consulting services.

Select Accounts Receivable > Common > Free text invoices > All free text invoices. On the Action Pane, click Free text invoice.

On the Action Pane, click Add Line, in the Description box, enter the service provided (e.g. Consulting), select the Main Account and enter the amount. It's not mandatory to enter Quantity and Unit price (this is a new functionality in AX 2012, see below).

Microsoft Dynamics AX 2012 includes many improvements to free text invoices, and introduces the following:

- Customer invoice correction process
- Recurring free text invoices
- Ability to enter quantities and unit prices on free text invoice lines
- Addition of a review (workflow) process for free text invoices

Customer invoice correction process

In Microsoft Dynamics AX 2009, correcting a free text invoice involved issuing a credit note against the incorrect customer invoice and creating a new customer invoice. In addition, you could not link the new customer invoice, corrected customer invoice, and customer credit note to one another.

In Microsoft Dynamics AX 2012, a new **Correct Invoice** button is added to the **Free text invoice details** form and the **Free text invoice** list page. A new form will open where the user can adjust the necessary information and then post the correction.

The process for correcting a free text invoice involves the following steps:

- The user clicks **Correct** on the **Free text invoice** form.
- The system creates a copy of the original free text invoice.
- The user makes changes to the copied free text invoice.
- The user posts the changes.
- The system creates a credit note and all the original settlements are reversed and reapplied to the new credit note.

- The system creates a link between the Corrected, Credited (Canceling), and Original customer invoice for a clear audit trail[21].

Recurring Free text invoice

In Microsoft Dynamics AX 2012, a new feature is introduced to let you set up a customer to be billed on a recurring basis. The new feature involves a three step process for enrolling a customer for a recurring free text invoice.

- Create a Free text invoice template. One template can be used for multiple customers. You can define templates from Accounts receivable > Setup > Free text invoice templates
- Assign the template to a customer. This step enrolls the customer; each customer can have multiple templates. You must specify a recurrence start date in the Billing start date and a Recurrence pattern.
- Generate and post the recurring invoice. Periodically generate an invoice based on the recurrence assigned at the customer level. The process can be set up as a batch process from Accounts receivable > Periodic > Recurring invoices > Generate recurring invoices.

The normal scenario is a monthly service agreement that is signed, where the service is charged on a monthly basis. User will use the recurring invoice template and assign it to the customer to automate the invoicing process.

Workflow for Free Text Invoice

The standard Microsoft Dynamics AX 2012 workflow framework is extended to work for free text invoices. This framework enables users to decide whether a review process should be required on free text invoices.

When a workflow configuration is enabled for free text invoices, the following tasks are possible:

- Designate who will be the approver(s) of the invoice;
- All free text invoices must be submitted by using the Submit button;
- Users can approve the invoice, request a change from the submitter, recall and resubmit the invoice, or reject the invoice;
- After the invoice is approved, the Post button becomes available;
- Optionally, user-defined tasks can be added to the workflow configuration.

---

[21] You can also use the new free text invoice workflow configuration to approve the change.

Free Text Invoice Quantities and Unit Price

Frequently, a free text invoice line can be used to sell a quantity of a kind of goods, services, or rights. Providing this information to the user and a basic amount calculation in Microsoft Dynamics AX 2012 will help better identify and explain charges to customers.

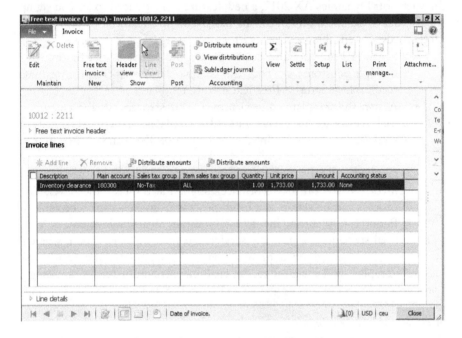

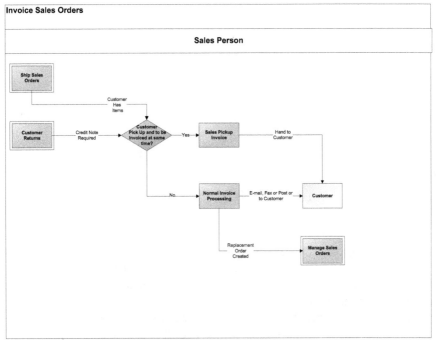

Source: Microsoft documentation

10 INVOICE PAYMENT

Microsoft Dynamics AX 2012 provides capabilities for processing a variety of payment and credit note needs. With customers linked across companies, payment processing can be consolidated into a single legal entity so that you can accept payments on behalf of all your companies.

In Microsoft Dynamics AX 2012, users are able to apply payments to invoice lines and set up payment prioritization policies that can be applied during the settlement process. These capabilities provide flexibility in prioritizing payments and better matching when receiving partial payments.

Microsoft Dynamics AX 2012 also includes:

- Credit card processing using Payment Services for Microsoft Dynamics ERP, allowing you to authorize sales order transactions and capture amounts at invoicing.
- Electronic payment processing using standard banking formats.
- Settlement priority that enables you to select how payments are applied to accounts receivables documents when automatic settlement is used.
- Flexible payment terms that allow you to control when payments are due and to schedule multiple payments to match the needs of your customers.
- Deposit slip integration with the banking module.
- Post-dated checks management for storing and releasing checks when they are due.
- Bills of exchange processing that allows you to draw bills of exchange and process remittances from your bank.

Settlement parameters

To access Settlement parameters, open Accounts Receivable > Setup > Accounts receivable parameters.

Partial payments can be applied to specific free text invoices and interest notes lines.

The following parameters are available in the Accounts receivable parameters form:

- Automatic settlement - Select this check box to automatically settle open transactions when a payment or credit note is updated. If this check box is cleared, users can settle accounts manually when entering payments or later by using the Settle open transactions form[22].

- Cash discount administration - Specify whether an obtainable cash discount difference is regarded as a cash discount difference or a payment on an account when an invoice is settled. This setting is used when the settled payment amount, which includes the cash discount, does not equal the amount of the invoice that is being settled. There are two possible values for this parameter:
  - Unspecific – The cash discount difference is handled in the following ways:
    - If the applicable cash discount is posted in the same legal entity as an overpayment, the cash discount amount is adjusted by the amount of the overpayment.
    - If the applicable cash discount is posted in a different legal entity as an overpayment, the customer cash discount account that is specified in the Accounts for automatic transactions form is used.
    - If the applicable cash discount is for an underpayment, the customer cash discount account that is specified in the Accounts for automatic transactions form is used.
    - If there are multiple cash discounts, for example if an overpayment is settled with multiple invoices, the adjustment to the discount is made from the last invoice that is settled to the first discount amount. The first discount is used when there is a tiered

---

[22] You can set up different options for each customer posting profile.

discount. For example, if the invoice is paid in five days, allow a 10% discount; if the invoice is paid in 15 days, allow a 6% discount. The overpayment is adjusted for the first tier of discount, which is 10%.

o Specific – Use the customer cash discount account that is specified in the Accounts for automatic transactions form.

For example, if we have an invoice with total amount 105.00 for which we can obtain a cash discount of 10.50, the amount to be paid, which includes cash discount is 94.50. If the customer actually pays 95.00, if Unspecific is selected in parameters, the invoice will be settled, and the difference of 0.50 will automatically be posted to the ledger account that is specified for cash discount differences. If you select Specific, the invoice will be settled, and the difference of 0.50 will automatically be posted to the sales ledger account as a payment.

- Maximum penny difference - Enter the maximum permitted penny difference for the settlement of accounts receivable transactions. If the penny difference is equal to or less than the penny difference that is specified in this field, the difference will be posted to the penny difference ledger account that is specified in the Accounts for automatic transactions form.
- Maximum overpayment or underpayment - Enter the amount that is accepted for overpayment and underpayment.
    - o If the overpayment or underpayment produces a penny difference that is less than the difference that is defined in the Maximum penny difference field, the penny difference amount is posted to the penny difference account.
    - o If the overpayment or underpayment produces a penny difference that is greater than the difference that is defined in the Maximum penny difference field, the penny difference amount is posted to the difference account that is selected for the Customer cash discount posting type in the Accounts for automatic transactions form[23].

---

[23] To calculate tax on overpayments or underpayments, in the General ledger parameters form, click Sales tax, and then select the Sales tax on overpayment or underpayment check box.

- Calculate cash discounts for partial payments - Select this check box to allow for discounts to be automatically calculated for partial payments.
- Calculate cash discounts for credit notes - Select this check box to allow for discounts to be automatically calculated for credit notes. In Accounts receivable, a credit note transaction is a negative transaction that has a value in the Invoice field in the Free text invoice form, or a return in the Sales order form.
- Mark lines on free text invoices and interest notes - Select this check box to enable the Mark invoice lines button in the Enter customer payments, payment Journal voucher, and Settle open transactions forms. This lets users mark individual lines for settlement. When this check box is selected, open transaction lines are created every time that an invoice that has an amount greater than zero is posted. Each new open transaction line represents a corresponding line from the original posted invoice. If the invoice references a payment schedule, open transaction lines are created for the invoice lines that make up each installment of the schedule. For example, an invoice that has four lines, and that is associated with a schedule that has four payments, would create 16 open transaction lines.
- Prioritize settlement - Select this check box to enable the Mark by priority button in the Enter customer payments and Settle open transactions forms so that users can assign the predetermined settlement order to transactions. After the default settlement order is applied to a transaction by using the Mark by priority button, the order and the payment allocation can be modified before posting.

For example, let's suppose company payments are settled based on the following priorities:
- Invoices are settled first.
- Payments are applied based on the invoice amounts starting with the smallest ones.

In the Accounts receivable parameters form, in the pane on the left, select Settlement. The parameter Mark lines on free text invoice and interest notes is selected so that transaction lines can be marked for settlement. Mark the Prioritize settlement option to define how transactions are prioritized for settlement and click Manage priority.

Select Transaction type, and then select the Active check box. The highest priorities have Invoices. Select Transaction amount and then mark the Active check box. Make sure that Sort order is set to Ascending. This means that the smallest invoices are settled first. Close the form.

Payment Journals

After you register, approve, and post the invoice, the customer must pay for the invoice. When you receive a customer payment, use the payment journal to register it.

You can use payment journals to do the following:

- Enter and post payments.

- Make and enter payments according to the terms of payment established with the customers. In the Payment journal, you can select the customer invoices to which payments will be recorded by creating the journal's payment lines:
  - o Use a Payment proposal to search for invoice lines that meet selected search criteria. For example, you must generate payment lines based on payment due dates.
  - o Use the Settlements option to select the specific invoice lines to settle, and to which to record payments.
  - o Create a Payment journal line manually to enter the payment details manually.

Payment Proposal

When customers make payments, you must create and post them in a payment journal, both to record the payments to the customer's accounts, and also to ensure that you can reconcile the Accounts Receivable information with General Ledger information. Use a payment proposal as an effective way to select the payment records and create the payment journal. The payment proposal does the following:

- Searches for payment lines that either are due or have a maximum date for receiving a cash discount.
- Checks open and approved customer transactions.

Only transactions with either a due date or a cash discount date are included in the search. As soon as the system generates payment lines, you can edit them in the payment journal[24].

Payment Journal - Notes on Generating Payments

Sometimes, customers allow the company to withdraw the payment directly from their bank accounts. In this case, use the generate payment functionality to withdraw the payment from the account. In these cases, when you create the payment journal, it is ready to be paid. The procedure on how to generate payments is the same for payment proposals, settlements, and manual payment journals.

Enter Customer Payments Form

An alternative to manual creation of Payment journal lines is the use of the Enter customer payments functionality. Use this form to enter, settle, and

---

[24] A red mark shows in the Is marked field if a transaction is already marked for settlement. You must enter a Customer account and Currency to use the Settlements option.

save customer payments. You can select Transactions based on the following fields:

- Customer account information
- Customer invoice information, including:
- Open invoice
- Credit note
- Collection letter

You also may view customer transaction records across multiple companies and define other aspects of the payment line, such as Method of payment, Offset account type, etc.

Enter Customer Payments Form

If the amount in the Amount field of the Enter customer payment form does not equal the total of the marked transactions, then the form will display the warning that the payment is not fully settled. Adjust the marked transactions[25] or amount accordingly. If you do transfer payment to the journal without adjustment, normal overpayment or underpayment posting rules apply.

Note: To clear any transactions marked for payment in the Enter customer payments form, click the Clear button.

Note: If the selected transaction is not an invoice transaction or credit note transaction, an asterisk will appear in the Invoice field of the created payment line.

Edit Open Transactions

Use the Settle open transactions form to make changes in transactions for customers. Only unapplied transactions are available for editing.
The following procedures explain how to:

- Settle invoices and payments
- Specify a cross rate between invoices and payments
- Reorganize transactions with new due dates

Settling Invoices and Payments

You can settle invoices and payments in the Settle open transaction form, if, for example, the invoice and payment are not settled when you create the payment.
The following information is relevant to settling invoices and payments:

---

[25] To view the details of the selected customer transaction, click the Show document button.

- If the amount paid is more than the amount due, the system settles the invoice and the payment transaction remains open for the amount by which the payment exceeded the amount due.

Note: If the over/underpayment feature is being used it can force them to be equal and close the transaction.

- If the payment amount is less than the amount due, the system subtracts the payment from the amount due and the invoice remains open.
- If the amount paid equals the amount due, the system generates a payment transaction for the payment amount, and then closes the transaction.

Reorganizing Open Transactions

You or a customer might pay one invoice on multiple dates or use multiple payment methods, such as a check and cash. When this happens, you can reorganize an invoice into several parts and assign a separate payment method to each part. After reorganizing the invoice, you can settle each new invoice line with a separate payment.

Consider the following information to reorganize customer transactions in accounts receivable journals and vendor transactions in accounts payable journals.

Note: You can also reorganize transactions in the general journal and in payment journals.

Placing an Accounts Receivable Transaction on Hold

To make data entry more flexible, you can enter a transaction on one date, and then put it on hold to prevent users from posting it until a specified date. This functionality is useful if you have an agreement with a customer about when a transaction can be posted.

To prevent a transaction from being posted until a specified date, enter a release date. The transaction is on hold until the release date occurs. You can edit and save transactions that are on hold, but you cannot post them unless you first remove the hold.

About Release Date for On Hold Transactions in Different Time Zones

If your organization includes users who work across different time zones, the date and time when a transaction is released from a hold is based on the time zone of the user who most recently modified the Release date value. Because the transactions release at midnight on the specified date in that user's time zone, the actual date and time of the release adjust accordingly for users in other time zones.

For example, on December 31 in New York, a user puts a transaction on hold at noon Eastern Time, and enters a release date of January 1 (the next day). The user sets up the transaction to be on hold until midnight Eastern Time, so the user must wait 12 hours for the transaction to be released.

Users in London, which is five hours ahead of New York, also must wait 12 hours. However, because the transaction was put on hold at 17:00 Greenwich Mean Time on December 31, the transaction will not be released until 05:00 Greenwich Mean Time on January 1.

For users in Seattle, which is three hours behind New York, the transaction was put on hold at 09:00 Pacific Time on December 31. When the transaction is released 12 hours later (at 21:00 Pacific Time), it will still be December 31 for these users.

Reverse Settlements

When you work with reverse settlements:

- Use the Closed-transaction editing window to edit fully applied or settled transactions that are in history.
- Use reverse settlements if the bank does not honor a payment, or if you used the wrong date or settlement amount.
- An unsettled invoice is considered unpaid and is handled together with collection letters.

Reimburse a Customer

Consider the following when you work with the reimbursement feature:

- Use it to repay customers who have credit amounts because of overpayment or credit notes.
- It transfers the balance to a vendor account. The vendor account is assigned in the Customer form, otherwise a one-time vendor account is created automatically.
- The Accounts Payable Coordinator can create an ordinary payment when the balance amount transfers to a vendor account.

Electronic Customer Payment

The two methods to record electronic customer payments are:

- The bank sends a file that contains customer payments.
- Instruct the bank to collect payments from customers according to certain specifications if an agreement exists with the customer.

Centralized Payments

Organizations that include multiple companies can create and manage payments by using a central company. This eliminates the need to enter the same transaction in multiple companies and saves time by streamlining the payment proposal process, the settlement process, open transaction editing, and closed transaction editing for cross-company payments.

In a centralized-payment organization, each operating company manages its own invoice information and payments are received or paid by a central company, which is known as the payment company. During the settlement process, the applicable due-to transactions and due-from transactions generate. For ledger transactions, users can specify which company within the organization will receive the realized gain or realized loss transactions, and how cash discount transactions that are related to a cross-company payment are handled.

Prepayments (Deposits)

Accounting practice in many countries or regions requires that prepayments or deposits from a customer or to a vendor are not posted to the usual summary accounts for the customer or vendor.

Instead, these prepayments are posted to special ledger accounts for prepayments.

When a sales order or purchase order is made, an invoice is issued to the customer or vendor. During payment of the invoice, the prepayment and sales tax prepayment on the prepayment ledger accounts are reversed.

To record prepayments from customers:

- Set up and post the prepayment to a different ledger account than the summary account for the customer. This is an accounting requirement in most countries or regions.
- Later, when an invoice is issued against this prepayment, allocate the invoice against the payment directly from the sales order, reversing the original posting of the prepayment on the prepayment account in the ledger.

Collections

When customers do not pay, Microsoft Dynamics AX 2012 helps you manage your collections efforts by providing tools to interact with customers, document collections activities, and take action when needed.

In Microsoft Dynamics AX 2012, a new collections form has been added which brings together information from 14 different forms into one single form enabling quicker access to information like balances, credit history and contact information. From this form, access to 31 forms is provided allowing the collections agent to easily access more information from a single place. Tasks, actions, events and activities can be created to help manage and document collection activities. Write offs and settlement actions can be taken quickly from a single screen.

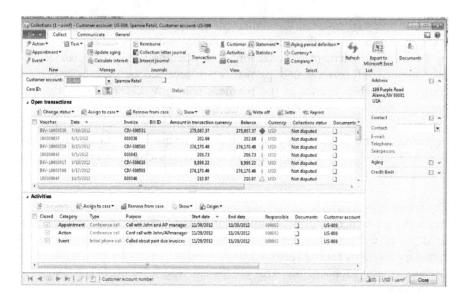

Aging periods

In Microsoft Dynamics AX 2012, use can select from a list of aging indicators to more easily identify accounts that are past due. When aging is defined, user can run a periodic job, the customer aging snapshot, that calculates and stores customer aging and collections information.

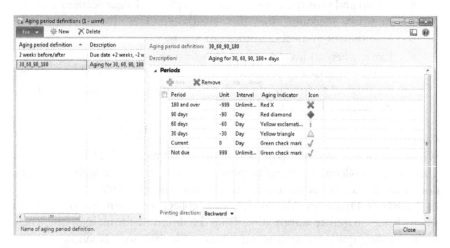

Customer Pools

Another available option for the user is to create customer pools to manage customers more efficiently. Customers and collection agents are assigned to a pool. This determines which customers a collection agent is managing.

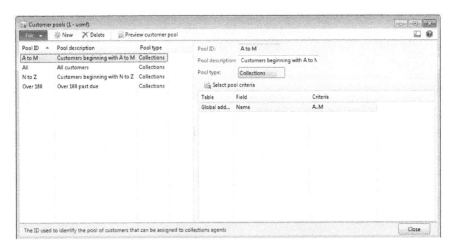

For example, user can create pools of customers based on criteria. These pools can then be assigned to employees. For example, a pool can include customers A-M and be assigned to an employee. If necessary, a pool can be easily reassigned to someone else.

Other functionalities
New functionalities of collections in Microsoft Dynamics AX 2012 include:

- Collections management list pages that provide key information about customers, their transactions, and their collections history.
- A collections form that brings together customer and financial information and allows you to:
- Log actions that have been taken and tasks that need to be performed.
- View and analyze all transactions, aged balances, and credit limits for a customer across all legal entities.
- Manage transactions and activities as a case to focus collection efforts.
- Send transactions and statements to customers in Microsoft Excel via Microsoft Outlook.
- Communicate by using email via Outlook.
- Collection letters that can be sent out in an escalating sequence to ensure that your requests receive the proper level of attention.
- Interest notes that assess fees and interest for customers that will not pay on time.
- Write-off functionality that helps you process uncollectible debts.

BIBLIOGRAPHY

Microsoft Dynamics AX 2012 Student Manuals

Andreas Luszczak - Using Microsoft Dynamics AX 2009; Vieweg+Teubner (2010)

Andreas Luszczak - Using Microsoft Dynamics AX 2012: Updated for Version R2; Springer Vieweg (2013)

Scott Hamilton - Discrete Manufacturing using Microsoft Dynamics AX 2012; Visions Inc. (2012)

https://informationsource.dynamics.com

http://technet.microsoft.com

Microsoft Dynamics AX 2012 Whitepapers

Microsoft Dynamics AX 2012 Help

ABOUT THE AUTHOR

Over 10 years of professional business experience with a wide variety of companies in different industries focusing on ERP implementations and training for Dynamics AX and Dynamics NAV, with responsibilities for ensuring that the full life cycle of a project is successful starting from customer requirements to development, testing, documentation, training, go-live and support.